"I saw the mov... Lombardi. The... the thought was the same: We're... a job, and each and every one of us will put everything we've got into getting the job done. That was Vince. Patton believed in reincarnation. Who knows? Maybe it was Patton who coached the Packers."

—Frank Gifford

Jerry Kramer played for the Green Bay Packers from 1958, one year before Vince Lombardi became head coach, through 1968, one year after Lombardi gave up the coaching job. In 1969, Mr. Kramer was voted the outstanding guard in the history of professional football. He is the author of two previous books, *Instant Replay* and *Farewell to Football*.

LOMBARDI
Winning Is the Only Thing
was originally published by
The World Publishing Company.

LOMBARDI

Winning Is
the Only Thing

Edited by

Jerry Kramer

PUBLISHED BY POCKET BOOKS NEW YORK

LOMBARDI: Winning Is the Only Thing

World edition published 1970

POCKET BOOK edition published October, 1971

7th printing.........................July, 1974

L

This POCKET BOOK edition includes every word contained
in the original, higher-priced edition. It is printed from
brand-new plates made from completely reset, clear, easy-to-
read type. POCKET BOOK editions are published by POCKET
BOOKS, a division of Simon & Schuster, Inc., 630 Fifth
Avenue, New York, N.Y. 10020. Trademarks registered
in the United States and other countries.

Standard Book Number: 671-78423-4.
Library of Congress Catalog Card Number: 74-128488.
This POCKET BOOK edition is published by arrangement with The
World Publishing Company.
Printed in the U.S.A.

ACKNOWLEDGMENTS

The editor would like to thank Edwina Louise, Dick Schaap and Don Forst, all of whom helped me set up interviews and ask questions; Bob Kamman, Mark Rosenweig, Arthur Woodard, Andy Carra and Toby Lubov, who typed the transcripts; and, most of all, each of the men who sat down to talk about Vince Lombardi.

FOR MARIE

Who told me that Instant Replay
should have been called Lombardi

FOR EVERYONE ELSE WHO LOVED VINCE
AND, ESPECIALLY,
FOR THOSE WHOSE LOSS WAS THE GREATEST—
THE PEOPLE WHO NEVER KNEW HIM

LOMBARDI

"Winning is not everything. It is the only thing."

"Like my father before me, I have a violent temper with which I have been struggling all my life, and with which I have had to effect a compromise. It is ineradicable, but it must not be irrational."

"I will demand a commitment to excellence and to victory, and that is what life is all about."

"Dancing is a contact sport. Football is a hitting sport."

"I think that a boy with talent has a moral obligation to fulfill it, and I will not relent on my own responsibility."

"Teams do not go physically flat, but they go mentally stale."

"Fatigue makes cowards of us all."

"The harder you work, the harder it is to surrender."

"The will to excel and the will to win, they endure. They are more important than any events that occasion them."

"*I hold it more important to have the players' confidence than their affection.*"

"*To play this game, you must have that fire in you, and there is nothing that stokes fire like hate.*"

"*The strength of the group is in the strength of the leader. Many mornings when I am worried or depressed, I have to give myself what is almost a pep talk, because I am not going before that ball club without being able to exude assurance. I must be the first believer, because there is no way you can hoodwink the players.*"

CONTENTS

Photographs appear following page 82.

LOMBARDI

INTRODUCTION

"There Was Nothing We Couldn't Lick When We Were Together"

He lay in his bed at Georgetown University Hospital, looking so drawn and tired, the intravenous needles feeding his right arm and hand. He motioned for me to come up on the left side of the bed. I went up to him and squeezed his hand, trying to say without words all the things I wanted to say, how much I had learned from him, how grateful I was, how much I loved him.

"Ouch," he said. "Don't break my hand."

And Vince Lombardi grinned, that grin that could lift you or warm you or dazzle you, that grin I had seen so many times in locker rooms and on sidelines, in meeting rooms and at banquets. That grin didn't belong in a hospital room. He didn't belong in a hospital room. If there were one indestructible man in this world, I would have bet anything it was Vincent Thomas Lombardi.

"It's good to see you, Coach," I said. "I've been worrying about you. I've been praying for you. My Mom asked me to tell you she's been praying for you."

Vince lay very still. "Jerry," he said, "I'm just so tired. I just can't see anybody, I just can't talk to anybody—not till I get this thing licked."

"I know, Coach," I said. "I know. I want you to rest. And give 'em hell."

I started to leave, but as I reached the door, Vince

called to me, "Hey, come here a minute." I walked back to him, and he turned to his nurse. "You think I've got a scar," Vince said. "You ought to see Jerry's scars. I'll tell you about them someday . . ."

And then his voice trailed off, he was so tired, and I held his hand again and said goodnight and walked out and wandered through the hospital, feeling depressed and vulnerable and lost.

It really is true, I thought. *It really is happening.* And I had a strange notion: I wanted to fight the cancer with him. I wanted to take the pain with him. Hell, together, we could lick it. Sure, we could. He'd taught me that. There was nothing we couldn't lick when we were together.

He died a month later. He died in September, only two weeks before the start of the 1970 football season, his time of year, the time of year when he did what he enjoyed most in all the world. He died in a deep coma, destroyed by intestinal cancer. He died, the most vibrant man I'd ever known, at the age of fifty-seven.

For a long time, I thought that Vince Lombardi was born at the age of forty-five, grinning and growling, demanding perfection, shouting, "Up . . . down . . . up . . . down . . . up . . . down." That was the only Vince Lombardi I knew—the man who built the Green Bay Packers, the man who turned us from an uninspired, losing football team into what I will always believe was the greatest football team there ever was.

No coach ever stamped himself so clearly upon a team —and no team ever recognized so vividly its debt to a coach. Even in the hottest days of summer, when he whipped us and prodded us and punished us, when he rode us so hard we all came together in our transient hatred for him, we knew that we were his creation, and we knew that the difference between being a good football team and a great football team was him and only him.

I spent eleven years in the National Football League,

nine of them under Vince, and I was always fascinated by him. I wondered sometimes what he was like at other stages of his life. Was he ever uncertain? Was he ever afraid? Was he ever dominated? I found it almost impossible to imagine Vince Lombardi when he was not in complete command of a situation.

I wondered, too, what emotions he aroused in the other people who knew him. I knew the emotions he aroused in me: Awe, love-hate, respect, gratitude and, certainly, fear. Very few things in life have frightened me, but Vince Lombardi did. Not physically, of course. I feared his disapproval.

When I decided in the fall of 1969 to work on this book, to assemble—partly out of curiosity—a composite portrait of Vince Lombardi, I had a moment of fear: I feared that he might disapprove of the project, and I knew that if he did, I would have to abandon it. Out of uniform, no longer under his gaze, I still could not go against him. For months, even as I began conducting interviews, I procrastinated, postponing a phone call or a visit to tell Vince about the idea.

Finally, in July, 1970, only a few days after his first operation, I called him at his home in Washington. "How are you, Coach?" I asked.

"Good, good," he said. "I bet I got a bigger scar than you, heh, heh, heh." He sounded perfectly healthy, perfectly strong.

"I'm working on a book about you," I said.

"I heard," he said. "I heard you're doing another one."

"I'd like to talk with you about it."

"I'll do anything you want," he said.

That knocked me out of my chair. I really didn't expect Vince to accept the project so cheerfully. He had been stung so many times he had grown wary of the printed word.

"I'd like to spend some time in training camp with you," I said. "Maybe I'll come down next week."

"You better wait," he said. "I'm still a little weak and

3

tired. But you call me in a week or two, and we'll get together."

A week or two later, he went back into the hospital. He never came out. We never got to spend that last training camp together.

In preparing this book, I explored Vince's background, of course, and I found that the basic facts of his childhood and young manhood gave little hint of the stature he was to gain: He was born in Brooklyn, in the Sheepshead Bay section, on June 11, 1913, the first of five children of Henry Lombardi, who had emigrated from Italy as a youngster, and his American-born wife, Matilda Izzo Lombardi.

As a teen-ager, Vince tried two dissimilar vocations. Hot-tempered and strong-fisted, he took a fling at boxing. He fought one bout, in the Golden Gloves, and won it, but took enough of a beating to realize that his future was not in boxing. Raised in a strict and religious atmosphere, he studied for the priesthood. Vince lasted longer at that than he did in the ring, but after two years at Brooklyn's Cathedral Prep, he decided that the priesthood was not for him. He switched to St. Francis Prep, where he starred as a fullback on the football team.

Then he went on to Fordham University, played guard on the football team, majored in business, achieved an excellent academic record and graduated in 1937, just as the country was starting to emerge from the Depression. Two years later, Vince became a football coach for the first time, at St. Cecilia High School in Englewood, New Jersey. By the end of World War II, in his middle thirties, he was still a high school coach, still totally unknown outside the Englewood area.

These are the facts, and they are neither spectacular nor startling. But the facts only scratch the surface of Vince Lombardi. As I discovered from talking to people who knew him in his formative years, he was already, down deep, the same man who in his early fifties would

4

dominate professional football, would be the biggest man in the biggest sport in the country.

This book consists of some two dozen interviews with people who knew Vince—mostly with men who coached with him and under him, and with men who played with him and under him. Each of the interviews was taped, transcribed, organized and condensed. They had to be condensed; some of them, in raw transcript, ran well beyond ten thousand words.

The first three interviews were with my three former Green Bay roommates—Jimmy Taylor, Don Chandler and Willie Davis. The first, with Jimmy, took place in New Orleans only a few days after the 1970 Super Bowl. Several other interviews—including the ones with Vince's super halfbacks, Frank Gifford and Paul Hornung—took place before Vince became sick; these interviews, naturally, show no concern for his health. A majority of the interviews were recorded during the nine weeks between Vince's first operation and his death, a period when mild concern turned too swiftly to sorrow; these sessions—Red Blaik's and Emlen Tunnell's, for instance—reflect an awareness of Vince's mortality. Only four interviews—with Vince's brother, Joe Lombardi; with his Fordham teammate, Leo Paquin; with his former assistant, Norb Hecker; and with his last superstar, Sonny Jurgensen—came after Vince died.

I conducted all of the interviews myself, except the ones with two former West Point football players, Bob St. Onge and Bob Mischak; the transcripts of these discussions were given to me. I hope that, in condensing and organizing, I have preserved fairly the views and emotions of all the interviewees.

What impressed me most, in talking with these men whose friendships with Vince spanned his lifetime, was the universality of respect for him. Purely because of this respect, busy men willingly gave up their time and rearranged their schedules so that they could offer me their recollections, their impressions. And these varied views gave me a perspective on Vince that I had never had. I discovered—as I had only suspected before—that he was a human being, not a god, that he had followed a fairly normal course of development. I could see where he had gotten some of his ideas and how he had formed some of his thinking. I could glimpse, but only glimpse, the sources of his incredible drive.

I've made my own feelings about Vince quite clear, I think, in two previous books, but still, in introductions and in brief postscripts to each of the following interviews, I couldn't resist adding a few of my own observations, a few of my own thoughts.

The last time I saw Vince, at Georgetown University Hospital, I spoke with Marie Lombardi, his wife, in the hallway outside his room. "Jerry," she said, "it's so hard to take."

I felt exactly the same way—helpless and frustrated—yet I tried to console Marie. "He's been so fortunate in his life," I said. "He's accomplished so much. And you've been fortunate. You've lived with him. Anyone who has spent even a day or two with him has been a little better for it."

There was so much more I should have said. I hope this book says some of it.

JOE LOMBARDI

"My Brother Can Beat Your Father"

Vincent Thomas Lombardi grew up in a comfortable home, a traditional Italian-American home where the father ruled and the mother served eight-course meals. Henry Lombardi, Vince's father, had not gotten past the sixth grade, but he spoke two languages and read everything he could, and he insisted that his three sons get the best possible education. Vince, the oldest, and Harold, the middle son, both went to Fordham University; so did several of their cousins. But when the youngest Lombardi son, Joseph, was ready to go to college, he didn't enter Fordham. Joe went to St. Bonaventure, for one simple reason: By then, Vince was the freshman football coach at Fordham.

"I wasn't going to go through that again," says Joe.

Joe Lombardi played four years of football under Vince at St. Cecilia High School in Englewood, New Jersey, and during those four years, he probably came to know his brother better than anyone else in the family did. Joe suffered under Vince, who leaned over backwards to show no favoritism, but he also learned.

"I may have resented him at the time," Joe says now, "but he was bringing something out of me, something more than I knew I had. He was making me into a man."

Vince also made Joe, who weighed barely 165 pounds, into an All-Metropolitan New York guard at St. Cecilia.

Joe was almost seventeen years younger than Vince, but, perhaps because of the life they shared on the football field, they were much closer than brothers that far apart in age usually are. When Joe got married, Vince was his best man, and later, when Joe went into the sporting goods business, Vince was one of his most demanding customers.

Joe Lombardi now works for the Rawlings Sporting Goods Company, and I met him for the first time at the wake for Vince. He reminded me so much of Vince, in his physical appearance, in his voice, especially in his gestures. At one point, he called me to him, to introduce me to his mother and father, and he cocked his finger, beckoning me, exactly as Vince had cocked his finger at me countless times.

A few weeks later, we sat down together, and during a conversation punctuated frequently with the familiar deep Lombardi laugh, Joe reminisced about his coach, his friend—his brother.

When I was a kid, Dad would tell Vince what to do, and then Vince would tell me and my brother and sisters. It was an old custom in Italian families: The eldest son gave the directions.

A lot of Dad rubbed off on Vince. Dad's a disciplinarian, too, and he's always been stubborn. He's eighty-three years old now, and he still walks to church for Mass every morning. He's not well, and the walk takes him a long time, but he won't let anyone help him.

Vince, being so much older than me, sometimes seemed more like a father than a brother. Once, when I was about eight or nine, one of the kids next door started yelling at me, the way kids do, "My father can beat your father," and I said, "Yeah, but my brother can beat your father."

I didn't exactly grow up with Vince, because he went

off to college when I was three and he got married when I was ten. I remember one time he brought home all the Fordham coaches and a few of the players for one of Mom's dinners, and while they were all laughing and talking and having fun, I sat at the top of the stairs and listened. Of course, I wasn't allowed to come downstairs.

Once I got to high school, I saw plenty of Vince, too much of him at times. At St. Cecilia, we didn't have a blocking sled for the football team. We had to hit Vin instead. Every guy on the club had to do it every day, and I was always the first to hit him and the last. That was his idea. I'd have pads on, and he'd be wearing a pair of shorts, and he'd look at me and say, "OK, hit me —on three."

And then he'd get down in his stance, and I'd get down in mine, and he'd say, "Ready . . . one . . ." And smack me.

It took me four years to catch on. My senior year, I got smart. I finally hit him first. And once I did, he called it quits. I never had to hit him again. He'd been waiting all that time for me to learn to beat him to the punch. He was happier about me hitting him than he'd even been about hitting me.

Oh, he was tough on me. He never let up. I was his brother. We used to scrimmage three days a week—Tuesdays, Wednesdays and Thursdays—and when I'd miss a block, he'd jump into the huddle and snap, "Who missed that block? Who missed that block?" His eyesight was miserable, but it wasn't *that* bad. He knew damn well who'd missed the block.

We used to play our games on Sundays, and every Sunday night, Mom would have dinner for the family, and Vin and Marie would come over. Vin would sit at one end of the table, and I'd sit at the other, as far away as I could get. I knew I'd made some mistake or other during the game, and each time I brought a bite up to my mouth, I'd be waiting for him to say something. He never did. I'll tell you, Mom's a great cook, but I never could eat much at those meals.

Once, during a game, I broke a metatarsal bone, and

9

Vince looked at me and said, "Forget it. There's nothing wrong with your foot." Our team doctor gave me a shot of novocain, and I played the rest of the game. Vince gave me the game ball afterward. That was my reward for playing with a broken metatarsal.

We always played our big game on Thanksgiving, against Englewood High School, and after the game Mom would give us a big Thanksgiving dinner. My junior year, the night before Thanksgiving, I was scrubbing and waxing the kitchen floor and the basement floor, getting them ready for the party, and I finished up a few minutes after ten. About ten-thirty, I was putting the pails and mops away, and Vince walked in the door. "You're not playing tomorrow," he said.

He had a rule that all his players had to be in bed by ten o'clock the night before a game, and that was it. It didn't make any difference what I was doing or why I was doing it, I'd broken the rule. And he stuck to it. I sat on the bench the whole game.

Vin liked to put a little razzle-dazzle in our offense, and one of his special plays was the guard-around. The guard would take a handoff from the quarterback and run with the ball. We'd use the play about three times a year and gain about sixty yards each time, and if anyone complained that it was illegal, that the guard wasn't a yard behind the line of scrimmage, Vin would just say, "Prove it." It was always the other guard who carried the ball, not me. Vince said I was too slow. He called me "Dragass," and wouldn't let me run with the ball. I was his brother is what it amounted to.

There were times I got so mad at him, I wouldn't speak to him. I'd answer him, "Yes, sir, no, sir," and that'd be it. But he was some football coach.

We had only about 500 students in the school, and maybe 125 were boys. But sometimes it seemed like most of the 125 were football players. Vince did a lot of recruiting, going from door to door in Englewood and neighboring towns to persuade big strong eighth graders to come to St. Cecilia. He had a wonderful way, especially with the parents.

Vince would use every psychological trick to get us up for our games. It was during World War II, and every now and then, before games, he'd read us telegrams from St. Cecilia graduates who were overseas, and then he'd tell us to go out and win the game for them. I don't know whether anyone ever really sent us telegrams or not. But I know Vin read them.

Once, we were playing Brooklyn Prep, and we knew we were in for a rough game. They outweighed us something like fifteen to twenty pounds a man. He got us together in the locker room before the game and gave each of us a pill and told us it would make us bigger. We believed him. We went out, feeling bigger and stronger, and beat Brooklyn Prep, 6–0. They were sugar pills, of course.

Just before another game against Brooklyn Prep, we all got postcards from the guys we were going to be facing. I got one from the opposing guard, telling me he was going to beat the hell out of me. Naturally, we got all fired up and went out and beat Brooklyn Prep again. Vince had written the postcards himself and had signed them and had gone to Brooklyn and had mailed them from there.

The week before our big game against Englewood High one year, he told us we were going to have a special secret practice. He got as many of our parents as he could to drive their cars up to our practice field one night—we didn't have lights—and form a circle and shine their headlights on the field. We thought we were really putting something over on Englewood High, a special, secret nighttime practice. There was nothing special about what we practiced, and there sure wasn't anything secret. Anybody could have driven up and watched. But it worked; we beat Englewood.

We had a kid on our team named Hook Cerutti, a swivel-hipped runner, which was why we called him Hook. Vin loved Hook, but, day in and day out, he beat Hook into the ground. He'd tear him down and chew him out, and then, every Sunday morning before our games, he'd call Hook into his office and talk to him alone. I never knew what Vince said in those sessions, but Hook always walked out ten feet tall.

Vince insisted that we play tough football, but clean football. Once, we played St. Mary's of Rutherford, New Jersey, and you could feel, even before the kickoff, that it was going to be a dirty, dirty football game. "If anybody raises a hand," Vin told us, "you're coming out." It was the dirtiest game I ever played in, but we listened to him. St. Mary's pulled every kind of dirty trick, but we played clean. At the end, my mouth was so bloody I couldn't eat right for two weeks. We won, and I would've liked to have heard what Vince said to the St. Mary's coach after the game. He was really steaming.

It wasn't enough I had Vince as a coach. I had him as a teacher, too, for physics and chemistry. He used to stand by the doorway, half-blocking it, and when a football player walked in, he'd say, "Had a lousy day yesterday, didn't you?" And then he'd give you his laugh, "Heh . . . heh . . . heh."

I wasn't the best student in the world, and sometimes I fooled around in class, and once, during chemistry hour, he made me come up and stand in front of the room while he was conducting some experiment. The experiment blew up, all over him and all over me, and, naturally, it was my fault.

He was a stern teacher. The kids were afraid of him. They shook when they found out they were going to be in one of his classes. He kept everybody's attention, he made sure of that. If your attention wandered, he'd throw an eraser or a piece of chalk at you, anything that was in his hands. He was a very basic teacher. He'd lay out all the facts very carefully, and the best part of his class would always be the last ten minutes, which he left free just to talk about the lesson, to let anybody who wanted to have his say.

God, he was busy in those days. He taught a full

schedule and he was the head coach in three sports—
football and basketball and baseball. He wasn't exactly
an innovative basketball coach. He wouldn't let anyone
shoot with one hand; everybody had to take two-hand set
shots. If anybody had ever tried a jump shot, he probably would've gone through the roof.

One famous basketball game, his opponents went into
a zone defense, so Vince had his guards stand out near
half-court and just pass the ball back and forth, freezing
it. I think they went almost a full half without either
team taking a shot. The final score was something like
3–2, his favor. But he wasn't stubborn, oh, no, not him.

In addition to his St. Cecilia chores, he was president
of the county coaches association and he officiated basketball, baseball and football games—with those eyes of his.
He liked nothing better than to have some coach come off
the bench and try to argue with him about a decision.
You can imagine how gently he reacted to that.

All through my high school football career, I don't
think Vince praised me once. He couldn't. But the praise
came with the All-Metropolitan team. He had to put me
in for that, and when I was selected, he went with me to
the All-Met dinner. He'd had other players named All-
Met before, but he'd never gone to the dinner. I think
that was my greatest thrill, having him come with me to
the dinner.

When I graduated from St. Cecilia, I was all set to go
to Fordham. And then they named Vin freshman coach,
and I decided I'd had enough of playing for my brother.
I went to St. Bonaventure, played football there as a freshman, then transferred to Fordham. As soon as I transferred, Fordham made Vince an assistant coach for the
varsity. That did it for me. I switched back to St. Bonaventure, and then, when Bonnies gave up football, I did,
too. I switched again, back to Fordham, and got my degree there.

Afterward, Vin and I were in the sporting goods business together for a while, and I saw him often when he
was an assistant coach with West Point and the Giants. I

remember he was approached about a lot of head coaching jobs—the Philadelphia Eagles, the Air Force Academy, a bunch of other colleges—but he kept waiting for the right spot and the right time. When he was offered the job in Green Bay, I guess all his friends advised against it. They told him the odds were too high against him. But he took it. He knew what he was doing.

When Vin moved to Washington with the Redskins, I was working for Rawlings, and the company asked me to go down to see if I could sell him some equipment. I made an appointment, just like any other salesman, and went down and showed him some uniforms. He liked them. "I want 'em in gold and burgundy," he said.

"They don't make athletic uniforms in burgundy," I told him. "You can have cardinal or scarlet or . . ."

"I want burgundy," he said.

There was no arguing with him. I took the order and wrote down, "Lombardi Burgundy." Then, underneath, in parentheses, I wrote, "Cardinal."

Late in May, he and Marie and my wife, Betty, and me and Vince Jr. and his wife, Jill, got together one night in New York. Vin was even more emotional than usual, talking about the family and about all the things he wanted to do, and when we came out of P. J. Clarke's, about four o'clock in the morning, he bought flowers for the girls. He was beaming. It was probably the most relaxed evening I'd ever spent with him. "He's never looked better," Betty said.

A month later, he went into the hospital. I prayed for him. We all did. I remembered what he once told me. "Never pray for victory," he said. "Pray for the will of God."

I suppose I shouldn't have been, but I was amazed by how closely Vince Lombardi, the high school coach, paralleled Vince Lombardi, the professional coach, down to his insistence—Joe told me—that every player show up for every meeting and every practice not on schedule, but ahead of schedule. In Green Bay, we lived in two time zones: Central Time and Lombardi Time, which ran fifteen minutes ahead of Central Time.

The incident with Joe and the metatarsal bone predated by more than twenty years Lionel Aldridge's broken leg in Green Bay, but Vince's reaction didn't change. "When are you gonna start running?" Vince yelled at Lionel, maybe four days after the cast came off. "That bone you broke is not a weight-bearing bone!"

His insistence upon observing the letter of his rules, his emphasis upon hard, but clean, football, his chewing out of a player and then building him up (I was Hook Cerutti two decades later), his psychological gimmicks—it was everything I knew about the man.

The only difference was that in Green Bay we had blocking sleds. We didn't have to hit Vince. It was just as well. I probably never would have learned to beat him to the punch.

15

ALEX WOJCIECHOWICZ

"He Was Ready to Kill Himself to Win"

Fordham University's Seven Blocks of Granite, probably the most famous line in the history of college football, were, in fact, Ten Blocks of Granite. Only four of them played regularly on both the once-beaten 1936 and unbeaten 1937 Fordham teams; three of the starters in 1936 were seniors—including Vince—and gave way to new men in 1937. The center on both lines, and an All-American both years, was Alex Wojciechowicz, who went on to spend thirteen seasons in the National Football League. Wojciechowicz, a sixty-minute man as a center and linebacker, was elected to the NFL Hall of Fame in 1968. Two years later, he and Vince were among the five charter members of the Fordham Hall of Fame.

Wojciechowicz works now for the State of New Jersey, and I saw him in August at his home in Atlantic Highlands on the Jersey Shore. "Isn't it something?" he said. "On May 16, the day we were inducted into the Fordham Hall of Fame, Vince was sitting right next to me for two and a half hours, jovial, laughing, not complaining about anything. And now—it's just a matter of days."

The first time I saw Vince Lombardi—I was a freshman, he was a sophomore—he didn't impress me as a top-notch athlete. He was very quiet and he wasn't very big. Of course, once I saw his fight and desire, I began to appreciate him.

It took Vince a while, too, to impress our head coach, Jim Crowley, and our line coach, Frank Leahy. Vince didn't play first-string in his sophomore year, but he was a regular guard the next two seasons.

He was the bravest guy I ever saw. He weighed between 170 and 180 pounds, and he usually faced guys who were 210 and 220. They were tough, too. We played the best teams in the country, teams from every section, Pittsburgh and Georgia and St. Mary's and Texas Christian.

We played our home games in the Polo Grounds, and the visiting teams—knowing they were in front of the New York press, the most influential press in the country—always played over their heads. We had some fantastic games. We played Pittsburgh three 0–0 ties in a row, 1935 through 1937, and in 1936 Pitt was ranked third in the country, and the next year they were national champions.

Vince went into every game with the attitude, "I'm here to die, are you?" He was ready to kill himself to win. He never said much, and he was a leader by example. One game, someone hit him in the mouth, and he played the whole sixty minutes, cut and bleeding, then went and got about twenty stitches in his mouth.

The younger players especially looked up to him. He was older than most of his teammates—he was twenty when he entered Fordham, almost twenty-four when he graduated—and he always seemed a little more mature, a little more confident of himself. He was an A-student, and he was never too busy to help out the other guys when they were having trouble with their courses. They'd go to Vince's room, and he'd tutor them. He was a good teacher even then.

I'll never forget how upset Vince was after the final game his senior year. We were undefeated, going up against New York University, and I don't believe NYU had won a game all season. We were supposed to kill them. There were a lot of reports going around that, after we beat NYU, we'd go to the Rose Bowl. In fact, some people had signs printed up saying: ROSE HILL TO ROSE BOWL. Rose Hill was the area in which Fordham was situated.

We went into that game so sure of ourselves, and we got beat, 7–6. We were all pretty disappointed—we wanted to dig a big hole and climb in it—but Vince took it the hardest. He knew it was his last chance to get into a bowl game, and for several days after the defeat, he just walked around without saying a word. Pitt went to the Rose Bowl in our place. We'd tied them, and they beat Washington in the Rose Bowl, 21–0.

After college, Vince was too small to go into pro ball, but he was such a good student of the game, he had to do something connected with football. I used to see him every now and then when there'd be a reunion of the Seven Blocks of Granite, and for a long time, I wondered when he was going to make his move, when he was going to stop coaching high school. I always knew he was going to be a success. The only question was when.

Alex Wojciechowicz's house is set on a hilltop looking out over the Atlantic. He designed the house himself, and he has a large, handsome den with a fireplace and a desk where he handles his chores as president of the NFL Alumni Association. He has a hedge of roses, which he tends, and a rock garden and a swimming pool and a telescope aimed at the ocean, and he seems to lead a very pleasant life. As I left his home, I couldn't help thinking that perhaps Vince had a place like this in mind, a place where someday, when he stopped pushing himself, when he stopped driving so hard, he could finally relax and enjoy himself and his family.

LEO PAQUIN

"He Had No Halo Over His Head"

Of all his Fordham teammates, probably none knew Vince so well as Leo Paquin. Like Vince, who finished high school late because of his two years at Cathedral Prep, Paquin entered Fordham at the age of twenty; he had lost one year working and another at prep school. Both came out for the freshman team as backs in 1933 and both were converted to linemen, Paquin to an end, Vince to a guard. They moved up to the varsity in 1934 and helped anchor the Seven Blocks of Granite in 1936. The summer before their senior year at Fordham, the two worked together at Manhattan Beach in Brooklyn, and Paquin lived with the Lombardis. Later, he and Vince played semi-pro football together, then coached against each other, Vince at St. Cecilia, Paquin at St. Francis Xavier in New York City.

Paquin is now athletic director at St. Francis Xavier, and two weeks after Vince's funeral, we met for breakfast at a Manhattan hotel. We traded a few football stories, and then I asked Leo Paquin about the reports I'd heard of a shower room brawl at Fordham.

It was on Wednesday, Bloody Wednesday—that was what we called our big scrimmage day—just before the St. Mary's game our senior year. We had a small shower

19

room just off our locker room. The main shower room was down the hall, but if you got in quickly after practice, if you were one of the first few, you could go in the small room and get showered and dressed and get back to your dorm fast.

On this particular day, Vinny and I were the first two into the small shower room. We'd both been in the scrimmage, and we were bruised and beat. A third fellow came into the shower. He hadn't been in the scrimmage; he wasn't a regular.

Just then, a fourth kid came up to the door of the shower room, a small, swarthy kid from Pennsylvania. There wasn't enough room for him to come in, so he waited by the door. This other fellow who was inside with Vinny and me called to the kid outside, "Hey, come here. Stand alongside Lombardi. I want to see which one of you looks more like a nigger."

That was all he had to say. Vinny's eyes began to blink—which was always the tip-off to his temper—and, boom, he threw a left hook. He caught the guy right in the nose. I was standing there, all soaped up, and I knew what was going to happen if they got caught fighting. I jumped in the middle, trying to break them up, and, boom, boom, Vinny threw punches right over me. He had a ring on, and he got the other kid in the mouth, and the blood started to spread.

The other kid was a strong kid, and he wasn't about to back off, so the two of them stood there, trading punches, and I just wanted to get them apart. They were both friends of mine, but I was more interested in protecting Vinny, because he was on the first team and we needed him against St. Mary's. "Quit it," I yelled, as the punches whistled in both directions. "If you get caught, you won't be able to play Saturday."

Finally, they stopped, and I started worrying about how to keep the fight quiet. I could hide Vinny—he was battered, but so was the whole first team on Bloody Wednesday—but the other kid was bleeding quite a bit. I took

20

him into the trainer's room, and I told the trainer, "Take care of this guy, will you. He slipped in the shower."

It was pretty obvious that if he had slipped in the shower, a couple of guys must've kicked him after he went down.

The word got out about the fight, and Jim Crowley suspended both of them. Crowley wasn't dumb, though. He only suspended Vinny until Friday afternoon; he was able to play Saturday. Jim suspended the other kid through the weekend, which didn't make any difference, because he wouldn't have gotten into the game, anyway.

Jim Crowley was one of the Four Horsemen at Notre Dame, and, naturally, he was in the Knute Rockne tradition of coaching, the go-out-and-win-this-one-for-the-Gipper school. He gave very emotional pep talks, and even though you'd hear the same lines every year, they'd work. Once he got going, someone had to open the door quickly, or we were going to go right through it.

Vinny probably got some of his ideas about pregame talks from Crowley, but I think his emotions were more part of his nature, more real. Crowley's emotions could be turned on and off as he needed them. That was the accepted style in those days.

It was quite a coaching staff we had. Under Crowley, we had Frank Leahy and Hughie Devore. Leahy, at Notre Dame, and Red Blaik, at Army, were the two most successful college coaches of the 1940s, and Hughie Devore coached Notre Dame while Leahy was in the service. Leahy was the expert on offensive technique—he got down in the dirt with the centers, guards and tackles, teaching them blocking—and he got most of the credit for the Seven Blocks of Granite. But, basically, we were a defensive unit, and Devore, who concentrated on our defense, never really got proper recognition. Crowley once told me, after I was out of school, that he never changed a single defense Hughie set up. Hughie taught me, and Vinny, too, that you had to establish yourself right away, preferably on the first play of the game. He taught me

21

to ram my head right into my man's numbers the opening play, and for the rest of the day, the guy was going to respect you.

I look back at Vinny at Fordham, and I guess what strikes me is that there wasn't any one special thing about him. He had no halo over his head, nothing that really set him apart from everybody else.

Football? He was a fine player, but he wasn't one of the best. He wasn't an All-American like Wojciechowicz or Ed Franco. Studies? He and I and Wellington Mara, whose father owned the Giants, had a running competition to see who got the highest grades, and we were all far above average, but there were smarter students than we were. The spiritual life? Vinny used to go to Mass every morning, but so did most of us. He wasn't the acolyte, so shiny that the priests fussed over him. Strong character? Certainly, Vinny was always a decent person, but he wasn't a saint. He enjoyed his occasional beer and he liked a good dice game as much as I did; he had no holier-than-thou attitude.

If you took these four categories—athletics, academics, religion, character—you wouldn't have put Vinny first in any of them. But what you'd notice if you looked carefully was that Vinny was among the top group in every category. Anybody else's name might appear near the top in one category or two, but he was up there in all of them. We just didn't notice it then. Vinny was just one of the boys.

Nobody ever pointed at him on the Fordham campus and said, you know, "There goes Lombardi," the way they did later in his life. At Fordham, none of us walked on hallowed ground.

In 1940, when Vinny was coaching St. Cecilia and I was coaching Xavier, we both signed up with a semi-pro club in Springfield, Massachusetts. The money looked pretty good, and we just worked out on our own during the week, then took a train up there at seven o'clock Sunday morning and played a game.

When we went up there for our first game, nobody bothered to tell us who we were playing. When we got there, we found out we were playing the New York Giants. We didn't do badly. We held the Giants to a 7–0 lead at halftime, and then they pulled away and beat us, 35–7.

Vinny didn't seem upset about playing against the Giants. What got him angry was what happened after the game. We knew we'd be taking the same train home we'd taken up in the morning, so we'd given one of the porters five dollars to buy some beer for the return trip.

Well, when we got back on the train, we waited and waited, and the beer didn't show up. Finally, fifteen or twenty minutes after we'd pulled out of Springfield, I spotted the porter. "Where's the beer you bought for us?" I asked.

"Oh, the boys are drinking it already," he said.

"Drinking it?" I said. "What boys? We're right here."

"You know," he said. "In the next car."

We walked up to the next car, and there were the Giants, finishing off our beer. I went over to Steve Owen, the Giant coach, whom I knew well, and said, "Steve, that's our beer. We paid for it."

"Geez," said Steve, "and I was just thinking what a great thing this was. We came up here to a little tank town and they treated us so well, even sending beer home with us."

By then, the beer was all gone, and Vinny sat there, looking very calm, but his eyes kept blinking all the way home.

Leo Paquin outlined the schedule the students followed at Fordham: They had to be in their rooms studying from seven thirty to ten o'clock every night, Monday through Friday; from ten to ten thirty, they could do whatever they wanted, as long as they didn't leave the dormitory; at ten thirty, their lights went out. When they became seniors, they were allowed to go out Wednesday nights, provided they were back in the dorm by ten thirty. It made training camp sound almost like a vacation.

Vince accepted the regimen, and he loved Fordham. He was a member of the school's board of trustees, and he valued the Insignis Award, presented to outstanding Fordham alumni, above any of his coach-of-the-year awards.

During the week that I met with Paquin, I couldn't resist a visit to the Fordham campus. I got lost at first—which is par for the course for me—roamed through the Bronx, passed the New York Botanical Gardens and arrived, purely by luck, at the Fordham campus. I drove through the gates, glanced at an old athletic field, saw aging buildings that reminded me of one of Vince's remarks—"A school without football," he said when his alma mater abandoned the sport, "is in danger of deteriorating into a medieval study hall"—then parked behind the gymnasium.

I entered the gym and wandered about. I found a small locker room, perhaps once the dressing room for the Seven Blocks of Granite. I looked for a football trophy case, but I saw only track and field trophies. I strolled outside the gym and sat on a stone railing, a spot where I imagined the Fordham football players of the 1930s must have sat while they waited for their buddies to emerge from the gym.

Across the way, a group of youngsters began playing touch football, and I watched them for a while. If I'd had a pair of sneakers, I would have gone over and joined them. I don't entirely understand why, but I wanted to touch a football on the Fordham campus.

MERV HYMAN

"His Image Was a Shell to Hide His Shyness"

After he graduated from college, magna cum laude, Vince attended Fordham Law School at night, worked during the day as an investigator for a finance company and kept in touch with football by playing on weekends for various semi-pro teams.

In 1939, he took a job as the assistant football coach at St. Cecilia High School. In addition to his football responsibilities, he coached the basketball team, helped coach the baseball team and taught Latin, algebra, physics and chemistry—all for a starting salary of $1,700 a year.

At St. Cecilia, Vince got to know Merv Hyman, who was then working for Time. *Hyman, four years younger than Vince, moonlighted as sports editor of a local weekly, the Englewood* Press, *covering, among other things, the athletic teams of St. Cecilia. The two young men, both bachelors, became close friends, and their friendship endured, even when one went west, to Green Bay, and the other went east, to* Sports Illustrated.

Today, Merv Hyman is the chief of research for Sports Illustrated.

I'd never met Merv Hyman, but I'd been told that I'd have no trouble recognizing him. He was out of his office

*when I arrived, on a Sunday late in August, and as I
waited for him, I studied the photos on his walls. It was
easy to spot Hyman: Just as I'd been told, he looks like
Vince, especially around the eyes and forehead.*

Then he came in and, in the middle of a hectic day—
Sports Illustrated *was wrapping up its pro football pre-
view—took a few hours to talk about Vince.*

It was funny the way Vince got into football. Nat
Pierce, who was the other guard on the Seven Blocks of
Granite, had been the coach at St. Cecilia, and after
three years he moved up to Fordham to be freshman
coach. Andy Palau, the quarterback behind the Seven
Blocks, replaced Pierce at St. Cecilia. Andy needed a line
coach, so he called up Jack Coffey, who was the athletic
director at Fordham, and asked who was around. Coffey
mentioned Vince.

Andy called Vince's home in Brooklyn, and his mother
answered the phone. "He's not here now," said Mrs.
Lombardi. "He's working for a finance company. What
do you want him for?"

"To coach football," Andy said.

"Coach football!" said Mrs. Lombardi. "Why would he
want to do anything as silly as that?"

Vince's father owned a successful wholesale meat business, and he would have liked to have had Vince come
in with him. But Vin had no interest in the meat business.

Eventually, Andy got in touch with Vince. "I'm head
coach out at St. Cecilia now," Andy said. "How'd you
like to be my line coach?"

"I don't know," Vince said. "I never really thought
about coaching football."

"Why don't you come out and we'll talk about it?"
Palau suggested.

Vince went out to Englewood, discussed the job with
Andy and decided to take it. There was one minor problem: Andy told him he'd also have to be the basketball
coach, and Vince didn't know too much about basketball.

Andy, who'd played basketball at Fordham, gave Vince a crash course in the sport, and Vince, of course, was a great student. He learned so well that, before he left St. Cecilia, his basketball team won the state championship.

Andy and Vince rented rooms in the same house in Englewood, and I was living in the town, and the three of us ended up spending a lot of time together. That first year, we were all bachelors, and I had the only car among us. We used to sit around and drink beer, and when we got twenty-two empty cans, we'd set up an offense and a defense and run through football plays. All Vince talked about, all he thought about, was football. You knew even then that one day he was going to be the best damn football coach in the country.

In 1942, Andy Palau replaced Nat Pierce as the freshman coach at Fordham—Nat went into the service—and Vince stepped up into Andy's job at St. Cecilia. Vince's first team lost one game, but then he went undefeated through thirty-two games.

In those years, most of the schools were using the straight-T offense. Vince used it—and improved on it. Sometimes, he put out a flanker; sometimes, he put a man in motion. He was an innovator, willing to experiment to make his team more effective.

Football, of course, isn't the same on the high school level as it is in college or the pros, but to Vince it was. He hated to lose. When he did, which wasn't very often, he took it hard. It was only a high school football game, but the way Vince acted, you'd have thought it was the end of the world.

In the beginning, I don't think he had enough patience with the kids who couldn't perform the way he wanted them to. He probably lost sight of the fact that these were only high school kids. If a kid couldn't excute a block right, Vince'd get right in there on all fours, not just telling him what to do, but showing him. He'd belt the hell out of some of these kids—he kept himself in good shape—and some of them would belt the hell out of him.

27

Vince was volatile. He was a shouter. In order to express himself, he had to shout. He felt that he had to bawl out the kids to make them better players and to strengthen the team, but I know, from our conversations, that it hurt him to do it.

He pushed those kids, but he loved them. Near the end of his years at St. Cecilia, he had a quarterback named Billy White, a fine young man who went on to Fordham and then into the service. He was killed in action in Korea. Vince was at West Point by then, but the death of the boy still devastated him.

Vince was always very emotional. He'd cry at the drop of a hat. He even used to cry when he won sometimes. The thing that most people don't understand is how shy he was. His image—his gruffness, his toughness—was always a shell to hide his shyness. I don't think he ever really enjoyed being the center of attention. He was more comfortable just being part of the crowd.

He was especially shy around women. He went with Marie for several years before they got married, but I don't know if he even had a girl friend before Marie. There were several girls in Englewood who were crazy about Vince, but he wouldn't give them a glance. He just wasn't interested. It might've been a different story if they could block or tackle.

He and Marie were married in 1940. I got married the following year, and I remember once, when the Lombardis had to be chaperons at a St. Cecilia dance, Vince asked my wife and me to go with them. "You gotta," he said. "What am I gonna do there with all those kids?"

"What am I gonna do?" I said.

"Oh, c'mon," he said. "We'll just stay a couple of hours and then we'll go out and have some drinks."

We went, and Vince kind of stood in the corner all night. Some of the kids asked Marie to dance, and she did, but Vince was the wallflower. I don't know what he would've done if one of the young girls had asked him to dance. He probably would've run. He didn't even dance with Marie. I'm not sure he knew how to dance.

I got to know Vince's parents a little over the years. His father is a tough old guy who has died, I guess, about eight times. I remember I was visiting my mother in the hospital in Englewood several years ago, and I met Mrs. Lombardi in the lobby. "What are you doing here?" I said.

"Well," she said, "Pop is sick. He's in bed upstairs. He feels read bad, and we don't think he'll last much longer."

I went in to see him. He was stretched out in bed with tubes and bottles all over the place. He looked as if he were gasping his last breath. About three days later, I stopped by again. He was up in a chair and yelling for the nurses to get him this and get him that. Just a tough old guy. He's had three or four heart attacks, but he always comes back.

Vince must have gotten his temper from his father, because his mother is a nice, sweet lady. The only time she would ever get angry was if you went to her house for dinner and, after the first eight courses, you said you couldn't eat any more.

I don't think Vince was ever unfair to anyone—at least not consciously. He accepted people or rejected them strictly on the basis of their individuality. There were no colors or races or religions. There wasn't a bigoted bone in his body.

A couple of years ago, we were doing a series of articles on the black athlete, and we wanted to know why Green Bay had been free of trouble. I knew why; knowing Vince, I knew why. I called him up and asked, "How many blacks do you have on your squad?"

"I don't know," Vince said. "I can tell you how many players I have on the squad. And I can tell you which ones aren't going to be here next year. But I can't tell you how many are black and how many are white. If you really want to know, I'll sit down and count them."

29

He was honest enough to add: "One thing that's helped us is that we've been winning. When you're losing, it's easy to have discontented players—black and white."

Vince told me that one of the reasons he stopped coaching in 1968 was that he found it increasingly difficult to deal with the players both on the field as the coach and in the front office as the general manager, particularly after the players formed their association. He was afraid that he'd have some rift with the player representative and that some resentment might carry over into the field —not in him, but in the players. I'd guess his feeling was that the rewards a man got from pro football were being a winner and being a good man, and the hell with the money.

I saw Vince late that year down in Miami, and I asked him, "Well, how's the season been?"

"Terrible," he said. "The worst year I've had in my life. I made a big mistake. I shouldn't have stopped coaching."

Vince shook his head. "Can you imagine *me* playing golf in the middle of the damn football season?" he said.

Merv Hyman mentioned that the Reverend Timothy Moore, who was the school's athletic director during the years Vince spent at St. Cecilia, had been close to Vince. A few days after Vince's funeral, Father Moore offered some of his memories.

Father Moore, in addition to his other duties, helped out as an assistant coach under Vince at St. Cecilia. "He was using his run-to-daylight idea even then," said the priest. "At the other schools, the players had to block one particular way, and the backs would go through a specific hole. Not Vince's team. It was the same as in Green Bay: The linemen could block either way, and the backs could go inside or outside, depending on where the hole was."

It was a struggle, Father Moore said, to keep Vince at St. Cecilia for eight years. "We knew how good he was,"

Father Moore said. "We could see his talent, his dedication. He was a wonderful teacher—whether he was teaching Latin or algebra or football. He was offered several coaching jobs in public high schools, but I wouldn't let him go. I talked him out of it every time. Then, in 1946, just before Vince went to Fordham, my brother Ray offered him a job. Ray was in the construction business, and Vince used to work for him during the summers. He was the best foreman Ray ever had. The workers idolized him. Ray offered Vince $15,000 a year to go into the construction business—and I was then paying him $3,500 a year. Vince was tempted, I suppose, but he turned it down. He was committed to football."

When Vince went on to professional football, he and Father Moore remained friends. "I was in the Redskins' camp with him last year," the priest said, "and one morning at breakfast, one of the people who helped out around camp walked up to him and said, 'Mr. Lombardi, could we postpone practice till nine thirty so that the boys can see the astronauts take off for the moon?'

"Vince thought it over and decided that it wouldn't do the astronauts or the Washington Redskins any good if he postponed practice. He turned down the request. Then he went out on the field with the team, and a couple of hours later, I saw Sam Huff, and Sam told me what had happened. 'He gave us a beautiful talk,' Sam said, 'and then we all knelt down on the field and prayed for the astronauts.'

"Sam smiled. 'We had some practice,' he said.

"That was typical of Vince: He didn't give up a minute of his practice, he got the boys thinking more seriously about the astronauts than if they'd watched the blast-off—and he still got a good workout out of them."

Father Moore's story reminded me of the time of the Cuban missile crisis—when President Kennedy set a deadline for the missiles to be dismantled. There was a good chance that if the Cubans and the Russians didn't meet the deadline, we'd be going to war. The deadline happened to fall during one of our practice sessions in

Green Bay, and somebody suggested to Vince that we postpone or cancel the workout. We were all pretty anxious.

"The hell with Cuba," said Vince. "Let's go to work."

We won the National Football League championship that year.

EARL H. (RED) BLAIK

"I Saw the Sparkle in His Eyes"

In 1947, after eight seasons at St. Cecilia High School, Vince became the freshman football coach at Fordham. The following year, he stepped up to become an assistant with the varsity. Then, in 1949, he made the most significant move of his coaching career: He accepted a post at West Point, as an assistant to Earl H. (Red) Blaik, the most successful college coach in the country.

West Point had been undefeated in four of the five previous seasons. The Army team had been national champions in 1944 and 1945. Before taking over at West Point in 1941 and reviving Army football, Blaik had spent seven years at Dartmouth and had turned a lackluster team into one that contended for national honors. Blaik—like Lombardi later—had a reputation for taking nothing and making something out of it. "The most important thing that ever happened to me in football," Vince once wrote, "was the opportunity to coach under Colonel Blaik. Whatever success I have had must be attributed to 'the old man.' He molded my methods and my whole approach to the game."

His first year at West Point, Vince coached the offensive line, and Army went undefeated and averaged forty points a game. In Green Bay, Vince often spoke to us of Colonel Blaik. Obviously, he was as awed by Blaik as we

*were by him. He made the Colonel sound so big that, in
my mind, I envisioned a man the size of King Kong.*

*In the summer of 1970, Colonel Blaik came east from
his California home to spend a few weeks seeing friends
and playing golf. I met him in his room at the Westchester
Country Club, and I was struck, immediately, by how
vibrant he looked and sounded. He wasn't quite King
Kong, but he was as trim and sturdy as any seventy-
three-year-old I'd ever seen. "I don't know what I should
call you, sir," I said. "Do you prefer 'Colonel' or 'Coach'
or 'Mr. Blaik'?"*

"Call me 'Red,' " he said.

*I mentioned that I was going to visit Vince the next
day. "The facts are so hard to take," said Red Blaik.
"You run across a man who's got that kind of vitality so
seldom in life. To think that he can't surmount this illness,
that he can't do anything about it—I can't accept it, that
in a month there may be no more Vince."*

*Colonel Blaik paused. "I spoke to him Sunday before
he went back into the hospital," he said, "and he told
me, 'I feel pretty good. I'm down to playing weight, and
I'm only running a low-grade fever. I'm coming along
pretty well.' "*

*The Colonel shook his head and began to recall the
days when the two of them were together at West Point.*

I'd never heard of Vince Lombardi in 1948. Sid Gillman, my line coach, was leaving to become head coach
at the University of Cincinnati, and I didn't know where
to turn for a replacement. I received many applications,
but I didn't like applications. Then a good friend of mine,
Tim Cohane, who was the sports editor of *Look,* told
me about this fellow down at Fordham who'd done a
good job with the freshman team. Tim thought this guy
was just great. I said I'd talk to him.

Frankly, I had no idea that I'd select him. He didn't
have the sort of background in coaching that would in-
dicate he was ready for the quality of football we played
at West Point. Vince couldn't have been more than thirty-

five or thirty-six, and he had a baby face. I'd never seen him play. I didn't know he was one of the Seven Blocks of Granite at Fordham.

But after talking to him for only a short time, I knew he was ready. He was ripe. I saw the sparkle in his eyes.

From our first brief conversation, I could tell that he had a good knowledge of the game, that he had much more than just an ordinary mentality, that he had an unusual amount of imagination. Right then, as a young fellow, he had that special quality of being able to electrify a room.

Vince had only one real shortcoming when he joined us. He didn't have the control of his emotions that he acquired later. His attitude at the beginning, I think, was, "They're all equal. Let's give 'em all hell." At first, the boys didn't understand him. They didn't understand his drive. I remember the first day of spring practice in 1949, he was standing talking to me, and somebody in his group, one of the linemen, did something wrong. The linemen were probably seventy-five feet away, and he dashed over there, screaming at the top of his lungs. I yelled, "Vince! Vince!"—and he pulled up like a race horse. He was explosive. He had a short fuse. Of course, he was still immature.

But he could overcome his immaturity because he had such a dynamic personality, so much youthful vitality. And, like me, he was captivated by the game of football. Once he got to playing around with circles and X's, he was in another world. This is the one thing about football that the ordinary layman doesn't understand at all: There's nothing that's comparable to the fascination of developing a football team. I'm not thinking about the boys —about developing them into men—I'm thinking about the game itself. How do you approach a season? How do you approach a game? How do you get people to play beyond their abilities? How do you get the most out of your material? How do you adjust your material to an opponent's material? How do you make the intelligent move, the decisive move, always under tremendous pressure?

35

The possibilities are endless, and a man with an inquisitive, searching mind, like Vince's, could see those possibilities and could devote a lifetime to coping with them.

Vince got into the habit of working sixteen and eighteen hours a day at West Point. He reported every morning at eight, the same hour I did, and often we'd work up past midnight. Some people say that's nuts. It may be, but if you have a job that's fun and fascinating, you can't spend too much time doing it. Just the other day, when Vince heard I might be coming down to Washington to visit him, he told a mutual friend of ours to ask me if I'd be interested in looking at some films with him. He knew the answer. If I were blind, I'd still be interested in looking at football films. In the five seasons Vince was with me at West Point, we must have spent three or four thousand hours together, looking at films.

We did a lot of things at West Point that Vince was able to incorporate into his later coaching. He said that himself, many times. In one way, we were very similar to the professional setup: We never practiced more than an hour and a half a day. We couldn't get our players for any longer than that the way the schedules were arranged at the Military Academy. We had to be well organized. We couldn't afford to waste any time. We had to know exactly what we wanted to teach our players every day.

We never got great athletes at West Point. Once in a while, we'd get some good ones, but most of the time, we had to develop our athletes. We had to get them to rise above their skills. We had to toughen them up mentally. And I suspect Vince did quite a bit of that in Green Bay, too. We had several sayings we followed, and one of them was, "You have to pay the price." That was my philosophy, and it was Vince's, too.

My respect for Vince grew every year, and our relationship developed into a very close one. He was coaching our offense when my son, Bob, was playing quarterback for us. That was a very difficult position for me, coaching my son, especially at the Military Academy, where you have so many things that inhibit the boys. Vince took over Bob and was a real buffer between us. And to this day, Bob worships Vince. Bob gets emotional about very few people, but he does about him.

Vince was with me when the cribbing scandal broke at West Point, when practically the entire football squad, including my son, was expelled. Next to me, Vince was probably the most deeply affected person. He was terribly, terribly broken up. Everything we'd built up, and everything we'd stood for, went right out the window in twenty-four hours. He, like myself, never forgave the people up there, the antifootball people who forced and magnified the whole situation. It was an asinine thing, sheer stupidity. They harmed a lot of young boys. They harmed the Military Academy, too.

He stayed with me during the next few difficult years, when we had to play with a totally inexperienced team, with a rinky-dink squad. We won only two games in 1951, only four the following season. Then, early in 1953, we went out to Northwestern and lost in the closing minutes. In the dressing room afterward, Vince was crying because one individual had made a mistake that cost the game for a bunch of kids who'd worked so hard coming from nowhere. We didn't lose another game that season. We went on to become Eastern champions, and Vince was even more proud of those boys than he was of our undefeated team in 1949. And so was I.

Vince and I were both so absorbed in our work that we didn't have much time for hobbies or recreation. But we did get to play golf every now and then. Vince was a lot like President Eisenhower on the golf course. Neither of them ever felt at home there. They both believed that every shot had to be perfect, and they were both always unhappy because they hit so few good ones. We had one hole at West Point, about 130 yards long, that used to drive Vince crazy. For some strange reason, every time he got to that hole, he shanked. The hole was on the side of a mountain, but it was just a straight, simple shot. Vince could get up and hit three balls on that hole, and he'd

37

shank all three. It never happened to him on any other hole. Whenever we'd come to that hole, we'd all start laughing. Except Vince. It burned him up. He never could understand why any ball he hit didn't go straight into the hole.

I don't think there's any doubt but that he would have been my successor had he stayed at West Point. He was certainly the most able of my assistants by 1954, the year he left to join the New York Giants. Before the Giants hired him, they came to see me. They'd been after me for a while to go with them as head coach, to succeed Steve Owen. Steve had been extremely popular with the newspapermen, and they felt they had to get someone who could overcome this. They wanted me for my coaching ability, but they also wanted me to get the heat off them. I kept turning them down, and, finally, Wellington Mara said to me, "Well, would you mind if we talked to Vince? We'd like to get him as an assistant coach."

"I'd hate to lose him," I said, but I told the Giants to go ahead, to approach him. Vince didn't like the idea of leaving West Point—he always had tremendous loyalty—but, of course, he had to take the offer from the Giants.

After he went to Green Bay, he used to call me fairly often—when he was down, when he felt the team wasn't responding. He'd ask me what I thought he should do, but I knew he didn't really want my advice. He just wanted to unload to me, because he knew that I understood the way he felt.

If I had to pick one reason for his enormous success, it would be that he has magnetism. This applies to almost all the great leaders, and Vince has certainly been a great leader. He may have learned a few things during our years together, but he didn't learn that magnetism at West Point. It was always in him. You don't put magnetism into people.

As I left his room, Red Blaik told me he had spoken to Vince on the telephone the previous day. "He holds the watch on the people who give him the cobalt treatments," Blaik said. "He counts off the two minutes they're supposed to give him."

It sounded so typical, so much like Vince, we both had to smile. "The last thing he told me," said Colonel Blaik, "was, 'I'm gonna lick this.'"

WEST POINTERS

"We Equate Him With What We Know Blaik Was"

Early in August, a day or two after visiting with Red Blaik, I went to Washington and wandered through the maze of the Pentagon to meet a group of men who had played for Vince and the Colonel at West Point. The meeting was set up in the office of Colonel Charles Kuyk, and we were joined by four other colonels: Dan Foldberg, Winfield Scott, Ben Davis and Irving Reed. All of them had played on Vince's first team at West Point, the unbeaten and untied 1949 team.

It was a reunion—at least one of the men had just been reassigned to the Pentagon and had not seen the others in years—and it was, also, a tribute to Vince that these men were willing to give up a few hours after their working day to talk about him.

What follows is a composite of the remarks of the five colonels. Obviously, not all of them agree completely with every sentence. But, generally, this is how they felt about life at West Point in the middle of the twentieth century.

We were fortunate. We played under the greatest coach that ever lived—Earl Blaik. Colonel Blaik always had brilliant assistants. Just during the few years we were there, his staff included Sid Gillman, Murray Warmath and Vince Lombardi. Within five years after we graduated, Gillman led the Los Angeles Rams to a divisional title in the National Football League, Warmath made Minnesota one of the top teams in the Big Ten and Lombardi revitalized the offense of the New York Giants.

We used to wonder whether Blaik hired these men and made them great coaches—or hired them because he could tell they were already great coaches. Certainly, all of them brought skill and energy to West Point, but they all learned a lot there, too. They didn't learn only from Colonel Blaik. They learned from each other. Gillman, for instance, was the man who brought the camera to West Point, who started filming our practice sessions. He also instituted the system of grading us for each game and posting the grades so that everyone could see them.

But Colonel Blaik was the master, no question about it. It was his team. He ran it, and his assistants assisted. He questioned them and he listened to them, but he made the decisions and they abided by them.

Colonel Blaik was a reserved man—cool, calm, controlled, even aloof. He was a great admirer of General Douglas MacArthur. He kept a picture of General MacArthur on the wall behind his desk, and when he talked to us before a game, he patterned his manner of speaking after General MacArthur's. Colonel Blaik never got too close to his players, perhaps because he realized that the guys come and go each year and it would break his heart if he became too attached to people. He was always utterly frank with us, utterly honest. He wasn't given to bawling us out—he left that to his assistants—and he wasn't quick to praise. But when he did praise you, that was enough to pump you up for weeks.

Gillman's personality was similar to Colonel Blaik's, but Lombardi's was different. He was much more effervescent. He'd cheer us when we did something right—"Ah, that was a good tackle," or "Great block!"—and he'd groan when we did something wrong. He was a volatile young coach, a bundle of energy, and he didn't hide his feelings. But, still, he didn't chew us out much. He wasn't a particularly blistering individual, not then. Even though he seemed emotional in contrast to Blaik and Gillman, he was more reserved in those early years at West Point than, apparently, he was later.

There was one thing that separated Vince from Colonel Blaik. With Blaik, the Academy came first, and football second. He wanted to make sure that every team he turned out was the best possible representative of the Military Academy. That's not to say that he didn't want to win—he wanted to win every single game—but he saw football as part of a larger purpose at West Point.

[*To support this point, Dan Foldberg, who was an All-American end in 1950, told the following story about a game Army played against Fordham in 1949, a game someone later called the bloodiest brawl ever staged outside Madison Square Garden:* Near the end of the first half, I got my teeth knocked out by a little halfback who gave me a strong elbow. For the rest of the game, I chased the guy all over the field. I wasn't going to let him get away with it. I wanted a whack at him. It was very frustrating because he knew I was after him and he was a lot quicker than me. I finally got within three yards of the guy and swung at him and missed by about three yards. The official called a fifteen-yard penalty on me. I went through all the dramatics. I threw up my hands. "What did I do?" I said. "If you'd hit him," said the official, "you would've killed him." And when I came off the field, Colonel Blaik came up to me and smashed me one real good. "I don't care if he knocked your teeth out," he said. "You're not gonna play that kind of ball for me!" *Army won the game, 35–0.*]

Lombardi's one goal was to make us the best football team in the world. He didn't care whether we were representing the Military Academy or Vassar. And that's not intended to be derogatory. Vince didn't stomp on the Academy. He respected the Academy. But football was his life. Even in those days, you could tell that he wanted, more than anything else, to be the world's best football coach.

Vince never tried to imitate Blaik. He took the best parts of Blaik—and of Gillman—that he could use within his own personality. Perfectionism, for example. Perfectionism was the Colonel's forte, and he placed tremendous emphasis on fundamentals. One of the sayings we used to hear was, "Football is played ninety percent above the shoulders and ten percent below." Fundamentals were the ten percent below the shoulders, and without them, you couldn't utilize the other ninety percent. Our practices were wonderfully organized—we used to split up into four separate groups: offensive backs, offensive linemen, defensive backs and defensive linemen—and we learned by repetition, doing the same things over and over until we executed them properly.

Another one of Colonel Blaik's sayings was, "Inches make the champion." In practice, if we missed a first down by five inches, Colonel Blaik would stop the scrimmage and point out that, by a few inches, we had just surrendered both the ball and the opportunity to score a touchdown and, by the same margin, we had given the other team an opportunity to score.

Blaik stressed second effort. He liked nothing better than to see a good downfield block.

You notice we keep talking about Blaik rather than Lombardi. That's because we equate Vince with what we know Blaik was. Vince carried on the Blaik tradition of coaching, the tradition we were part of—the idea of being both an outstanding football coach and an outstanding individual.

None of the five West Pointers could recall specific incidents involving Vince—after all, twenty years had elapsed since they played for him, and he was overshadowed then by Red Blaik—but what struck me most about their conversation was that, in describing the Army teams of 1949 and 1950, they could have been describing the Green Bay Packers a decade later. I don't know

43

how many times I saw Vince run out on our practice field when we had missed a first down or a touchdown by inches. "Mister!" he'd scream at the ballcarrier. "This is a game of inches. I don't ever want to see you stopped by inches again. If you get this close and you don't make it, I'm gonna come out and kick your butt!"

Perfectionism, fundamentals, second effort, practice movies, game grades—all of these things were part of our regular routine in Green Bay, and I never even imagined that Vince might have picked them up from someone else. Of course, I always had trouble envisioning Vince as an assistant to anyone.

In separate interviews, two other West Pointers offered their views of Vince Lombardi. One was Bob St. Onge, who did not play under Vince, but served with him under Blaik as an assistant line coach.

St. Onge, who played on Army's Blanchard-and-Davis teams of the middle 1940s, admired Vince's deep religious convictions ("I went on a lot of trips with him, and he always took his rosary, and he never missed Mass") and his sincerity ("Everything he said came from the heart"), mentioned that Vince and Marie were the godparents of his twin sons and spoke of Vince's fiercely competitive nature. "The assistant coaches played a lot of handball up at West Point," St. Onge said. "We'd play doubles, and, usually, we'd have one very good player and one fairly good player on each side. Vince was the fairly good player on his team. He was a little older than most of us, and his legs weren't too strong. But nobody ever out-hustled him. Nobody wanted to win more." St. Onge said he had always believed, and hoped, that Vince would succeed Earl Blaik at West Point and that nothing would have been better for Army football. "If Vince had any weakness," St. Onge said, "it was that he sometimes got impatient with the players, with the rest of the staff, even with the head coach. When he was trying to sell one of his ideas, and Colonel Blaik would turn it down, he would

44

get a little downhearted and impatient. But he never challenged Colonel Blaik's decision."

The other ex-Army man was Bob Mischak, who was recruited for West Point by Vince in 1950, played under him from 1951 through 1953 and then, after his military tour, played under him again on the New York Giants in 1958. Mischak later played several seasons with the Oakland Raiders in the American Football League. He now coaches the line at West Point.

Mischak respected Coach Lombardi, he said, mostly for his organizational ability and his emphasis upon perfection. He was grateful to Vince for helping him switch from defensive end to offensive guard in 1958, a change which made him a more effective football player and prolonged his professional career. He gave Vince credit, too, for making him think like a winner, for getting him to believe in himself. When he went to work for AT&T, the telephone people, before becoming a coach at West Point, Mischak found that the principles Vince had instilled in him—organization, perfectionism, dedication, confidence—were as effective in business as in football.

But, still, Mischak could see flaws in Vince.

He's not that sensitive to people. He demands of you more than you think you're capable of giving, and while this technique works with many people, it doesn't work with everyone. For instance, he tried to make me as intense as he was, and I just wasn't that type. He overlooked my natural personality. I think I could have been a better football player for him had he taken my personality more into consideration.

To an extent, you had to completely conform your own personality to his, or you were wiped out. I know of instances where, because of his intensity, he lost good players. In 1958, he had Don Maynard with the Giants, and Maynard was a sensitive young man. Lombardi had him as a running back. Now, looking back, it's easy to see that Maynard, with his speed and his hands, was playing the wrong position. Subconsciously, I think, Maynard didn't want to be a runner; he wanted to use his ability, one against one, to get free. But Vince wanted him to be a runner, and he tried his normal approach, pitting his own will against the kid's, yelling at him and screaming at him, hoping that this would turn the kid around. It didn't. Maynard faltered with the Giants. He went on to become a great pass receiver, of course, with the Jets.

I remember another incident with the Giants. We were in training camp at Bear Mountain, and a young fellow named John McMullen was trying out for the team at guard, the same position I was involved in. John was a high-strung individual, and he was very concerned about making the team. On one hot day, Coach Lombardi, in his intense way, asked him about his duties on a particular play, and John just drew a blank. Vince started to yell at him, and John could find his salvation only in yelling back at Vince. The battle ended the following day. John left camp. That was it.

Vince sometimes had no patience. At a meeting one day in the Giants' camp, he was trying to convey something to the rookies, and he seemed to expect us to have the same knowledge he possessed. We didn't. He got furious. He ranted and raved and screamed, and we couldn't follow his point, and for a while, he just wasn't teaching. But then he caught himself, calmed down and started a new attack on the problem until we absorbed it.

It was never easy for Vince to control himself. At West Point, when we were practicing away from Colonel Blaik, Vince could be very demanding, very harsh. His true personality came out. But when Colonel Blaik would come close, Vince would become, "Yes sir, no sir, yes sir." He controlled his intense personality and conformed to the head coach (to the point where we players used to mimic him sometimes). I don't blame him for that. I do the same thing myself as an assistant coach. You have to. You are part of an organization. You are part of a society.

When I came to West Point a few years ago, I tried to imitate Lombardi's method. He was the most successful coach in the country, and it was only natural, since I had played under him, that I should try his style, his very dogmatic, intense approach. It didn't work for me. Eventually, I realized—as Vince himself has pointed out in his books—that you can't take another man's personality and coach with that personality. So I decided I had to be myself—perhaps a little more understanding, a little more tolerant. I would like to think I could still have similar results.

I think I understand Vince. I come from the same sort of background as his—strong people, a family where you accepted orders, where you did things without questioning them. If you were told to beat your head against the wall, you did it, and your father simply said it was good for you, and that was enough. I think we're entering a different period now. I think we now have to give youngsters a good reason to get them to beat their heads against a wall. The youngsters today are challenging the dogmatic approach to everything. We have to respond to that challenge. We have to adjust to it.

Could Vince? I don't know.

I can see Mischak's point of view, and I disagree with him strongly only on his assumption that Vince was not sensitive to people. I think he was. I think he was brilliant at reading different personalities. But I suspect that Vince sometimes sacrificed his own sensitivity, as he sacrificed so many things, to his larger goal, his pursuit of excellence and victory.

SID GILLMAN

"He Does What Everyone Else Does—Only Better"

After talking to Colonel Blaik and the West Pointers who played under him, I decided I ought to speak to Sid Gillman. I wanted to talk to Gillman because it seemed to me that he had exerted considerable influence, either directly or indirectly, upon Vince's coaching techniques.

Gillman has influenced many coaches: Ara Parseghian, Paul Dietzel and Al Davis, among others, served under him. He has been called "the master of organization— the best in the business." Before he went to West Point, he was head coach at Miami of Ohio, the school that turns out football coaches—Red Blaik, Paul Brown, Weeb Ewbank, Parseghian and Dietzel all went there—the way MIT turns out engineers. After his Army tour, he was head coach at the University of Cincinnati. In 1955, he took over the Los Angeles Rams and promptly won the Western Conference championship of the National Football League. Five years later, he became head coach of the San Diego (then Los Angeles) Chargers and promptly won the Western championship of the American Football League. Some people consider Gillman the force that got the AFL off the ground.

Sid Gillman is now the general manager of the Chargers, and I met with him in August in his office in San Diego. I told him that the West Point players had credited *him with introducing practice films and game grades at the Military Academy and that Vince had brought those ideas to the Green Bay Packers.*

I don't know how much Vince might have learned from me. After all, we never worked together on the field. Our association has been strictly talk; we both like to sit down and talk football. The year before Vince took the job at West Point, when I was still the line coach there, he used to come up once or twice every week, and we'd sit around and discuss football. I wish now I'd spent more time with Vince back in those days just so I could have figured out what made him tick.

As far as describing Vince as a coach, I wouldn't call him flamboyant or spectacular. He works hard, of course —he drives himself—but I'd say the things he does are what everyone else does, only he does them a little better. He's got great knowledge of football, and he's got the ability to impart that knowledge, and any time you put those two things together, you've got a helluva football coach. Vince also had great players in Green Bay. That didn't hurt him any.

Not too many people know it, but I helped Vince get the Green Bay job. I was attending an NFL draft meeting in 1958—I was with the Rams then and Vince was with the Giants—and as I came out of one of the sessions, a few of the Green Bay people happened to be standing around. I knew one of the Green Bay directors, and he started telling me how hard they were searching for a new coach.

"Why don't you contact Vince Lombardi?" I said.

I'd seen Vince a lot during the middle-1950s because whenever the Giants came to Los Angeles, he stayed at my place, and whenever we went to New York, I stayed at his. I knew that he wanted to get out on his own. He was in his forties then, and he'd never been a head coach anywhere except in high school.

The fellow from Green Bay said he'd love to talk to Vince, and he got in touch with him, and that was it.

49

I was glad to see Vince do so well. I've always liked him. Some coaches, I never go out of my way to see; if I happen to run into them, OK. But I'm always happy to see Vince. He's a great individual. He's got a great love for the game.

Not long after I visited with Gillman, someone showed me a copy of the 1961 San Diego Chargers' yearbook. The Gillman biography in that book began: "Winning isn't everything to Coach Sid Gillman. It's the only thing."

It seems I'd heard that somewhere before.

FRANK GIFFORD

"I Was Always Trying to Please Him"

When Vince joined the New York Giants in 1954, he walked into a disaster area. Their defense was a shambles; their offense was worse. The year before, they had lost nine out of twelve games and had scored only 179 points, the fewest of any team in the league. Vince immediately molded a new offense and, in the process, created a superstar: Frank Gifford, a halfback who could run, block, pass and catch passes.

An All-American at the University of Southern California, Gifford had been used almost exclusively on defense in 1952, his rookie season. Under Vince, he became the most exciting offensive halfback in the National Football League. In each of the five years he played for Vince, Gifford was nominated for the Pro Bowl. In those five years, the Giants never had a losing record, never scored fewer than 246 points.

I played against Frank in the 1962 NFL championship —we beat the Giants, 16–7—and I had admired him even back in my high school days, when he was one of the stars of the Pacific Coast Conference. But I never met him until early in 1964.

We had just played Cleveland in the runner-up game in Miami—"A game for losers played by losers," Vince called it—and afterward a bunch of us boarded a plane

*heading toward Los Angeles and the Pro Bowl. On the
plane, I got into a card game with Jesse Whittenton, my
teammate, and a few Cleveland Browns and Frank.*

*After about half an hour of playing cards, I turned to
Jesse. "Hey," I said, "didn't Frank Gifford get on this
plane? I'd like to meet him."*

*"Dummy," said Jesse, "you're playing cards with him."
He nodded at Gifford.*

*I'd thought that Frank was Frank Ryan, the quarter-
back from Cleveland. It was another brilliant moment in
the life of an offensive lineman.*

*In the spring of 1970, before we knew of Vince's ill-
ness, I sat down with Frank Gifford in his office at CBS.
After thirteen seasons with the Giants, Frank is now a
highly successful television sportscaster, covering everything from the Masters to the Super Bowl.*

*Frank mentioned that in 1953, the year before Vince's
arrival, he had played both offense and defense for the
Giants, averaging some fifty minutes a game.*

"I didn't realize that," I said.

"Well," said Frank, kindly, "you were just a kid."

*I guess I was. I was entering the University of Idaho
the year Gifford and Lombardi got together.*

After our miserable season in 1953, after the club fired
Steve Owen and promoted Jim Lee Howell to head
coach, I heard about Howell hiring some guy from Army
named Vince Lombardi to handle our offense. I didn't
know anything about him except his name.

When I showed up at our training camp in 1954, in
Salem, Oregon, Vinny was standing in front of the en-
trance to our dorm. He had that smile of his on his face,
and Jim Lee Howell was standing next to him. They
looked like Mutt and Jeff. Jim Lee was six feet five.

The first thing Vinny said to me was, "Hi, Frank,
you're my halfback." He'd been studying the movies, and
he'd made up his mind I was going to play strictly offense.

52

And that settled it. I never even looked at defense after that.

To be honest, very few of the guys liked him at first. For one thing, he had us running like we had never run before. But the main thing was that we resented a guy coming in from college and telling us what to do. And he was completely in charge. Jim Lee never interfered; he left the offense entirely to Vinny and the defense entirely to Tom Landry. As Jim Lee himself said many times, "I'm just here to take the roll and blow up the balls."

The first two or three weeks, we weren't too impressed by Vinny's Here's-how-we-did-it-at-St.-Cecilia-High-or-at-Army attitude.

One of the things Vinny did right away was put in the split-T option play, where the quarterback comes down the line of scrimmage and either pitches out or runs with the ball. Well, that may be fine with a college quarterback, who's young and strong and fearless, but we had Charlie Conerly playing quarterback. Charlie must've been about thirty-eight then—no, not really; more like thirty-three, but a tired thirty-three—and he didn't go for that running stuff. Charlie was willing to run the option play—just as long as we were practicing without pads. But he forgot about it when we scrimmaged, and he sure wasn't going to try it in a game. When we played our first exhibition, Vinny went through a big thing telling Charlie when to use the play and how to use it, and, of course, Charlie never called it once all night. He wasn't going to get himself killed. At the end of the game, Vinny walked off the field looking totally dejected.

But it didn't take us long to realize that even though Vinny's approach to football was very basic—fundamentals: hit, block and tackle—he was somebody special. His enthusiasm, his spirit, was infectious. We really began to dig him when he started coming up to our rooms at night after he'd put in a new play during a chalk talk. I was rooming with Charlie, and Vinny'd come to our room, after putting in an off-tackle play, and say, "Well, what do you think? Will it work?" He was very honest. When he put in the power sweep, he'd ask, "Can the halfback get down and hold that defensive end and stop the penetration?" That was my job on one side and Alex Webster's on the other. We'd say, "Oh, sure, Coach, we can do it." And then he'd just drill the hell out of us.

I can remember sneaking out some nights after curfew in Oregon, and sometimes I'd come back in pretty late, and the lights would still be on in his room. I realized then the kind of work he was putting in. He had to be exhausted, but he never showed it. He'd be out on the field the next day, going full speed, driving himself every minute.

We never feared Vinny in New York. It wasn't like in Green Bay later, when he came in with you guys as a winner, as an established person. To us, he was just an assistant coach from Army and St. Cecilia High. There were maybe twelve or fifteen of us who were the core of the offense, and we were kind of a clique, and Vinny liked to hang around with us. He'd eat dinner with us on the road and laugh with us when we won and die with us when we lost. We used to tease him and raise hell with him. We'd hide his baseball cap, things like that, just to see him get his emotions worked up. When he was showing us films, we used to bait him, lead him on to the point where he'd smash a table or throw an eraser at the blackboard. He'd break two or three projectors a year when he got angry. Once, one of the guys dug up an old picture of the Seven Blocks of Granite. We all cracked up at the picture, the way the old linemen used to squat down, looking like frogs. We used to play a game called Sports Quiz—you know, one guy would imitate a famous athlete, and the rest of us would try to guess who he was —and one day, our entire offensive squatted down like a bunch of frogs and yelled, "Sports Quiz, Sports Quiz." Vinny laughed, too.

He was always a great psychologist, great at analyzing individuals, knowing which players needed to be driven and which ones needed a friendly pat on the fanny. When he was with us, we had a few players who needed driving.

54

One was Mel Triplett. Mel used to exasperate Vinny. He could've been a great player—he had a fantastic year in 1956—but he never played up to his potential, except on certain occasions, like against the Cleveland Browns after they got Jimmy Brown. Mel always felt that he was better than Jimmy. You and I both know that he wasn't, but he was a fine football player.

Vinny used to ride Mel pretty good, especially in the movies. You know how he is with that projector. You could miss a block, and he'd never say a word sometimes, but he'd run the film back and forth, back and forth, till every guy in the room felt like he'd done something wrong. It was sort of like going to a revival meeting. A preacher will fire some buckshot out there, and everybody is going to feel it. Everybody is the guilty party.

Well, Mel used to think that Vinny was persecuting him something awful. All he really was trying to do was help Mel along. But one time he went a little too far with Mel, who was kind of a frightening guy when he got hot. Vinny kept running this one play back and forth, back and forth, back and forth—with Mel missing a block— and about the eighth or tenth time, Mel said, loud and hard, "Move on with that projector."

You could have heard a pin drop. We all wondered what was going to happen. Mel had told the rest of us a few times what he intended to do to Mr. Lombardi some- day. And Mel was the kind of guy who was emotional and might do just what he said he would. He was at the break- ing point right then. Vince didn't say a word. He went on to the next play. He read Mel just right. They never did have a confrontation. I heard a lot of guys over the years say they were going to punch Vinny out at the end of the season, but no one ever did. You've got to end up loving a guy who can build a team, put it all together— and you share in the rewards. But Vinny walked a very dangerous line at times.

He ruled us all equally—with one exception. He loved Charlie Conerly. He never said a harsh word to Charlie. And, again, he was really getting the proper reading, because Charlie didn't need it. You couldn't fire Charlie up with a branding iron. But you couldn't cool him off, either. Charlie was his own person.

When Charlie used to throw a couple of interceptions or blow an automatic—which really fried Vinny—Vinny wouldn't say a word. He'd get on Don Heinrich—Don was our other quarterback, and he was a little younger and a little wilder than Charlie—but never to the point where he got totally angry. I think he has a special fondness for his quarterbacks. A quarterback is his own extension on the field. I think he looked at Bart Starr as Vinny Lombardi out there. I think he feels the same way about Sonny Jurgensen.

But the rest of us got equal treatment. I remember when he put in the nutcracker drill: A defensive lineman sets himself in between two big bags, and an offensive lineman tries to lead a ballcarrier through. Everybody always used to say, "Oh, that poor offensive lineman." Nobody ever thought about the poor offensive back, who was just getting the hell knocked out of him. After an hour of banging heads, those defensive linemen were so hot and so mad they didn't care what they did to you. Maybe you were a star, or thought you were a star, but you ran the nutcracker as often as the rookie trying to make the team. Vinny kept track of it, close track, and if you tried to get out of one run at it, his teeth'd be grinning at you, and he'd be yelling, "Get in here, get in here," and there'd be no way you could escape.

Vinny had to be a tremendous influence on me, probably the biggest influence of my life, even more than my own father. I was in my early twenties when Vinny got me, and those were vital years for me. I was trying to prove myself and I wanted, more than anything else, Vinny's approval.

It goes back to my childhood. My family was always moving around, and I was switching from school to school. I was always the new boy, and I was always looking for acceptance. I wasn't a very brilliant student; I couldn't have been. But I could run and jump and catch a ball and hit a ball. Somehow, I realized that this was my entrée to the social structure of the particular school I was attending, whether it was in Wink, Texas, or Santa Maria, California, or twenty other places. All of a sudden, I was accepted by the "in" group in school just because I was the best halfback.

And yet I always doubted myself. I'll never forget the time Murray Olderman, the sports editor of Newspaper Enterprise Association, called me up and told me I was the most valuable player in the NFL. I laughed at him. I was way up in the standings in rushing, in pass receiving and in scoring, but to me it just seemed like an absolute stroke of luck that all this had happened. I felt the same way in college. I really didn't think I should have been an All-American. I really didn't think I should have been All-Valley in high school. As a pro, I was constantly worried about losing my job. I came back in 1957, the most valuable player in the League, and I saw the crop of rookies coming in and I was positive some guy was going to take away my job. Call it insecurity or anything you want, but that's what I was like. That's what drove me.

And Vinny could put his finger on these elements in a personality. He knew exactly how to motivate. He knew just what buttons to push. You see, I didn't hide anything from him. I was always just as open as I could be with him, because I liked him so much. I know that after a while it got to the point where I was playing football for just one reason: I was always trying to please him. When we played a game, I could care less about the headlines on Monday. All I wanted was to be able to walk into the meeting Tuesday morning and have Vinny give me that big grin and pat me on the fanny and let me know that I was doing what he wanted me to do. A lot of our guys felt that way. We had guys who would run through a stadium wall for him—and then maybe cuss him in the next breath. He had his favorites, and I'm proud that I was one of them, that I still am one of them.

I wasn't the kind of player who needed to be reprimanded, and Vinny understood that. But Jim Lee used to get on me. He felt I was a Hollywood star; in fact, he referred to me as the Hollywood Star, the kid from California who was getting too big for his hat. He hurt my feelings really bad a couple of times. Once, in 1957, against Cleveland, I missed a block. I went off my assignment, and Vinny chewed my fanny out right on the field, and it was forgotten. Then, the following Tuesday, Jim Lee picked it up again. He gave us a little lecture about how some of our big heroes had gotten too big for the game.

I walked out of that meeting with tears streaming down my face. I already felt bad enough—my missed block probably cost us the game—and Jim Lee made me feel worse. We were working out at Fordham, and I went and sat by myself by the pool up there. I was thinking seriously about chucking the whole thing, about quitting football. A bunch of people wanted to make a movie star out of me, anyway. Maybe Jim Lee was right.

Vinny found me. He sat down and we talked a long time. I knew I'd goofed up his play, goofed up his chance to win, and he knew how badly I felt about it. We talked about the play. I told him what I hadn't had time to tell him on the field. It was a splitout to the left, and I was supposed to come cracking down on the linebacker. But I got out too far, and the linebacker penetrated. I let him go, figuring the guard would pick him up, and I turned up field to block the safety. The guard got knocked off, and the linebacker damn near killed Webster. I made a mistake. I had no excuse.

We sat and talked about the kind of year we were going to have, and Vinny got me feeling better. He said something to the effect that this was his ball club, even though he wasn't the head coach. I think he felt that, in criticizing me, Jim Lee had gotten into an area he shouldn't have. I don't think there was any great affection between them, yet I never heard Vinny say anything but kind words about Jim Lee. Incidentally, Vinny was never really close to Tom Landry, either. But they had a great deal of respect for each other. Vinny learned a lot from Landry. I think he learned all his theories of defense from Tom. I don't know where else he could've learned it, because he sure didn't know anything about defense when he joined us.

I can remember very clearly the happiest I've ever seen Vinny. It wasn't after a game. It was in the middle of a week during the 1956 season. We'd gotten up over .500 in 1954 and 1955, but we hadn't finished first or second in our division. Then, in 1956, we won four of our first five games, and on a Wednesday—we were getting ready to play Pittsburgh—he called us all around him, the whole offense. He just couldn't restrain himself. He was bubbling. He was bursting with pride. "By God," he said, "we've really got something going." His eyes were shining. He just felt that we were going to win everything, and he knew it was his baby, and he had to tell us, and, of course, he was right. We did go on to win everything that year.

Once, just once, I saw him frightened. It was before the first Super Bowl game. I don't think you guys realized some of the feelings involved in that game. I don't think you guys felt any particular animosity toward Kansas City. But the owners, the NFL owners, really resented the AFL owners, resented the AFL barging in on their play, and they wanted blood. The coaches—some of them—felt this, too. It came down from management.

The Super Bowl was a CBS–NBC simulcast, and I was opening the show. My job was to set the stage. It was thirty seconds before air time, and I was down on the Coliseum floor and our director said to me, "OK, Giff, make it good. We got about seventy million." And it dawned on me right then how big this whole thing had gotten. It hit me, and I got weak-kneed. I was supposed to make a few opening remarks, talk a little with Vinny and then turn it over to Paul Christman and Hank Stram. My big fear was that Vinny was going to forget about it or just say, "Oh, the hell with it." I wouldn't have blamed him if he hadn't shown up. He had other things on his mind. But he came over to me right on time, and because it was so noisy, I had to get as close to him as possible. I put my arm around him, and he was shaking. He was actually shaking. That hit me harder than anything else. Here he was, the number one coach in football, perhaps the number one of all time, and on the floor of the stadium, before the biggest game pro football had ever played, he was trembling. After we got off the air, he said to me, "I'm afraid of this one." He had nothing to be afraid of—you guys won easily—but I think it scared him that he was representing a fifty-year-old institution against a bunch of upstarts.

People are always asking me what makes Vince Lombardi different from other coaches, and I've got one answer: He can get that extra ten percent out of an individual. Multiply ten percent times forty men on a team times fourteen games a season—and you're going to win. He proved that last year at Washington. That's not a talented team, and, my God, they hadn't had a winning team since 1955. But he made them winners. He made them believe they could win. Sonny Jurgensen loved him. He had no right to succeed in Washington. There are twenty-six teams now, not twelve like there were when he went to Green Bay. It's a hell of a lot harder to find good ballplayers. You can't trade the way you used to; you can't draft the way you could. There just isn't the same material available for every team. And the quality of coaching has been upgraded throughout the league. And, still, he did it. Nobody else could've done it. There are four or five coaches that know as much strategically and tactically as Lombardi, but they don't get that extra ten percent.

Vinny believes in the Spartan life, the total self-sacrifice, and to succeed and reach the pinnacle that he has, you've got to be that way. You've got to have total dedication. The hours you put in on a job can't even be considered. The job is to be done, and if it takes a hundred hours, you give it a hundred hours. If it takes fifteen minutes, you give it fifteen minutes. I saw the movie, *Patton,* and it was Vince Lombardi. The situation was different, but the thought was the same: We're here to do a job, and each and every one of us will put everything we've got into getting the job done. That was Vince. Patton believed in reincarnation. Who knows? Maybe it was Patton who coached the Packers.

You and me—we grew up believing in Lombardi's way of life, but I'm not sure that it's the answer for everybody. I'm not criticizing it, but for me to say that everyone should lead a Spartan life, well, I just can't do that. For a football player, or a soldier, his way of life is going to make you a winner. But I don't think you can apply it to every phase of society.

Still, I'd like my son to play for Vince Lombardi. I think if half the world played for Vince, we'd all live in a better place. I want my kids to grow up to be like Vince, to be as honest and dedicated as he is, not necessarily in the same direction.

The kids are different today. They weigh success differently than you or I do and certainly than Vince Lombardi does. I see it with my own kids and with the kids I talk to. By and large, they're competitive, but not competitive the way you have to be playing football. It's not important to them to go out and work themselves to the point of exhaustion to condition a body to be able to play a football game. Vinny's doctrine of self-sacrifice and dedication is fine for the Washington Redskins, but it would be a tough thing to get across to Scarsdale High School or Bakersfield High School. Those kids don't look at it like the whole world is going to fall apart if you don't beat the Bears.

Kids today don't fight like we did. They can play football and basketball like hell, but they're very gentle, very kind. They're out playing for fun, and it's not going to interefere with their demonstration for the week or with the things they consider important. If you took the football team from Scarsdale High or Bakersfield and dropped them under Lombardi, they might say, "What the hell is he talking about?" They wouldn't understand.

When I was a kid, I used to lie awake all night before a track meet or a football game, worrying, wondering. I used to cry when I lost a game, any kind of game. Now my son is playing football on an undefeated high school team—he was All-County this past year—and the night before a big game, I asked him where they were playing the next day. He didn't know. He didn't know whether it was a home game or an away game. He took his gal out the night before the game.

Football's going to change, too, but by the time it does, Vinny'll be out of it. I don't think he'll coach more than three or maybe four more years. I think he'll probably end up in government or heading a foundation or something. He's a fantastic organizer. He could join any major corporation, and within two or three months, he could be running the organization better than any man who grew up in it. He's got that knack. He's brilliant. He's something special.

It surprised me to hear Frank say that he played mainly for Vince's approval. I played to please Vince, too, but I had to. As an offensive lineman, I played a position where the general public often couldn't tell what I was doing right—or what I was doing wrong. I needed Vince to judge me. I never thought a player of Gifford's stature —of his acclaim—would feel the same way.

KYLE ROTE

"He Was Searching for a Relationship With Us"

During Vince's years with the New York Giants, Kyle Rote was more than one of his stars: He was Vince's kind of ballplayer. Kyle had a bad left knee that forced him, after a few pro seasons, to forget about playing half-back, to give up the brilliant running and passing that had made him college football's most spectacular All-American in 1950. He became a flanker instead and, through hard work and despite his painful knee, made himself one of the finest receivers in the league.

Rote was also one of the most popular Giants, and half a dozen of his teammates, including Frank Gifford, named sons "Kyle," a tribute that was never paid a later Giant hero, the quarterback, Yelberton Abraham Tittle.

Kyle and his knee lasted eleven seasons in the National Football League. He retired in 1962, helped coach the Giants for a while, then went into the broadcasting business. Now, after a decade as teammates, he and Frank Gifford are friendly rivals. While Gifford works for CBS in New York, Rote works for NBC. We got together in a restaurant near his office late in the spring of 1970, and Kyle volunteered his recollections of Vince.

You may find this hard to believe, but Vince Lombardi

impressed me as a shy person when he first came to the Giants.

When I look back at those days now, I suppose that I mistook caution for shyness. Vinny was a perfectionist, and to his credit, I think he wanted to make sure his feet were on solid ground before he asserted himself. He was feeling his way until he was positive of what he was doing.

His previous experience had been limited to high school and college football, and in his first exhibition season with the pros, Vinny was rather careful in his dealings with the players, especially the older players. I don't mean he was timid, but I do think he was searching for a relationship with us that would make us both feel acceptable to each other. He was perceptive enough to sense that, because of the absence of any arena for physical give and take, it's often more difficult for a rookie coach to be accepted by the veterans than it is for a rookie player.

Some of us tested Vinny in his first few weeks. Charlie Conerly and I were not above trying to play as little as possible in the preseason games, and I can recall Vinny, during one exhibition, coming to Conerly and me on the sidelines and asking if we thought we'd like to get in a little work. "Maybe in a couple of more series, Coach," we replied.

What Vinny didn't realize—or, at least, what we thought he didn't realize—was that Charlie and I were trying to pick our spot. We knew that before the game was over, we'd have to go in, and we were studying the opposing team's rookie defensive backs, trying to find one with a weakness we could take advantage of.

Fortunately for Charlie and me, we were usually able to find what we were looking for, and when we felt our club was in good field position, we'd tell Vinny we were ready. In we'd go, and more times than not, we were able to complete a pass on the rookie we'd been watching.

I honestly think Vinny, at the beginning, held most of

the older players in slight awe, and when we'd pull off a stunt like that, it enhanced his image of us.

Of course, that was only the first few weeks. After a while, Vinny would turn to us and say, "You and Charlie ready to go in now?"

"Give us just a few more downs," I'd say.

"Go in there now," he'd say.

The shyness or the cautiousness wore off quickly, and as Vinny began to realize that pro ball is actually a less complicated game than college ball—that the tactics and skills of the opposition are much more predictable—the Lombardi confidence began to emerge. And in direct ratio to the emergence of his confidence, our little "confidence game" submerged.

Vinny was close to us players with the Giants. We used to play golf with him and with the late Jack Mara, who was then the president of the team, and once in a while, we used to go to his house for dinner and for a few beers. He was relaxed with us.

One year, when we were training at Bear Mountain, New York, we lost most of our exhibition games, and Vinny decided that we were too tight. So just before our opening game, when Jim Lee Howell, our head coach, was off scouting or something, Vinny threw a beer blast for the whole team in the basement of the Bear Mountain Inn. We all loosened up, and we went on to win the Eastern championship.

You can respect a man without personally liking him, but I don't think you can personally like a man without respecting him. Count me among those who personally liked Vince Lombardi.

Kyle's mention of the beer blast and of how much Vince enjoyed being with the Giant players made me think of how difficult it must have been for him to divorce himself from the players in Green Bay. I think he really would have liked to have been close to us—I think he felt, as

I did, that the special appeal of football was the camara-derie among men with a common goal—but he knew he couldn't allow himself that luxury. To fulfill his commit-ment to victory, he had to go against his nature and stay aloof from us.

I remember how much he enjoyed Rookie Night, the one night when we all really relaxed together, when the rookies staged a show and made fun of training camp in general and of Vince in particular. They could be pretty rough in their caricatures, and they portrayed Vince as a dictator, and they ridiculed his manner and his physical appearance, and he sat and watched and laughed as heartily as anyone. It took a big man, and a strong man, to see himself through others' eyes, to see his foibles exposed and attacked, but Vince seemed to love it. He would have liked more opportunities to relax and laugh with his players, but he knew, in Green Bay, he couldn't be one of the boys anymore. He wasn't an assistant coach anymore. He had to be a leader.

EMLEN TUNNELL

"You Had to Walk Proud When You Were With Him"

When Vince left the New York Giants and moved to Green Bay as head coach and general manager in 1959, he brought along one Giant player—Emlen Tunnell, a thirty-six-year-old defensive halfback who had already served eleven seasons in the National Football League.

Em played three years in Green Bay, long enough to share in the first of our five world championships, and even in his late thirties, he was one of the finest defensive backs in pro football. I'll never forget one play he made: We were facing the Chicago Bears, and as they started a sweep against us, Stan Jones, their All-Pro guard, pulled and went to block Em. Jones was a weightlifter, one of the strongest men in the league, and he must have outweighed Emlen by forty pounds. Em brought up an elbow—a clean, crisp blow—and knocked him unconscious. They had to carry Jones off the field on a stretcher. That was the hardest I ever saw a defensive back hit an offensive lineman.

Emlen was Vince's kind of football player, Vince's kind of man. Before the 1960 season, there were some stories in the papers saying that Em probably was going to be playing second team. I asked him how he felt about those stories, and Em said, "The hell with that. My legs are *good, and I've got a big heart, and that's all you need to play this game."*

In 1967, Emlen Tunnell became the first of my Green Bay teammates to be elected to the Professional Football Hall of Game.

Emlen is now the defensive backfield coach for the New York Giants, and early one morning in August, I joined him for breakfast at C. W. Post College, the Giants' preseason headquarters on Long Island. I hadn't seen Em in a couple of years, but he was still as enthusiastic, as eager as he'd been the first day I met him in Green Bay. While we walked from the dormitory to the dining hall, he told me about the excitement of his induction into the Hall of Fame. "You know, Jerry," he said, "I always felt I was the best there was, but still, being out there, with all those great players, it was something. I'll tell you, I cried, I couldn't help it."

Then we went into the dining hall and, in a room filled with healthy young football players, Emlen talked about Vince.

If he was to come in here now, God bless him, while all these guys were eating, they'd all stop and stare at him. They wouldn't do that for anybody else. Hell, he's earned it. There's nobody else like him. Nobody else even close.

It's funny. I've been out of playing football a while now, and I can't remember about all the other coaches I played for, but I can remember about him. I won't say he was the best coach I every played under—'cause, who knows who's the best—but he was the most respected coach I ever played under.

I wouldn't have gone to Green Bay if it wasn't for him. I was old and tired then, and, you know, we always used to kid about Green Bay. We called it Siberia. It was like a threat: You look out, or you're going to get sent to Green Bay. They weren't winning then; they were just about the worst football team around. What was that saying? If you were caught out after midnight, you turned into a Green Bay pumpkin?

See, nobody else wanted me then. The Giants had told me I didn't fit into their plans for 1959. Well, hell, I suppose I could've hooked on with lots of teams if I'd tried, and I know they'd have taken me in Philadelphia, 'cause it was my home town, but Vinny kept calling me and saying, "Come on out here. You got nothing to lose. If you don't like it, you don't have to stay."

So I went out and spent three or four days with him, and he said, "C'mon, Emlen, you can help me out." I didn't want to let him down. I'd known him a long time —even before he came to the Giants, we used to train at Bear Mountain, near West Point, and I met him then —and I'd only turned him down once. That was when we were short of running backs with the Giants, and Vinny asked me if I'd like to play offense, and I said, "No, thanks, I'll stick to defense."

I told him I'd play in Green Bay, and when I moved out there for training camp, I talked with him about the racial thing. I was single, and there were no black girls out there, and he said, "Emlen, if you meet some girl you like, that's your business. I'm not going to tell you anything, and nobody else is going to either." Which was nice of him to say. Then he gave me that laugh of his—that "heh, heh, heh"—and said, "But, remember, Emlen, you're too old to be messing around with a whole bunch of girls." And he was right about that, too, you know.

When I got there, Nate Borden, the only black player in Green Bay before me, was living in a place where you wouldn't keep your dog. Vinny—I guess I was the only guy in Green Bay who called him Vinny—found out about it and made Nate move and gave the people who rented him the place hell. He found Nate a decent place to live. Vinny didn't go for any kind of prejudice. I remember the first day of practice, he said, "If I ever hear anyone using any racial epithets around here like nigger or dago or Jew, you're gone, I don't care who you are."

Green Bay wasn't too hip about things like that when

I first got there. I used to go into a lot of bars, just 'cause I liked to, and people used to ask me to compare Green Bay and New York, and I'd say, "Man, there ain't no comparison." And there wasn't, not for me, not then. In one place once, a lady yelled at me, "You no-good nigger, if you don't like Green Bay, why don't you go home?" That was the only hassle like that I ever had out there. And when I got ready to retire, the same woman came up to me and said, "Emlen, I'm sorry, I was wrong." Vinny turned that whole town around. He did it.

Vinny knew from the beginning what he was going to do in Green Bay. That first year, he told me, "Emlen, just stay with me, and I'm gonna build a dynasty here, heh, heh, heh."

He knew that right off he had to get some discipline, and he got it. He scared the heck out of everybody, even me. He had a rule during training camp that you had to be in bed with your clothes off and your lights out at eleven o'clock. The first Wednesday night we had off, I walked into the dorm at one minute to eleven, and he was standing in the hallway. "Hey," he said, "that's fifty dollars."

"Man," I said, "it's not eleven o'clock yet."

And he said, "Emlen, you know you can't be in bed with your clothes off by eleven."

He was right. I laughed, and he laughed that big hearty laugh of his, the one that made you feel good inside. But I still had to pay him the fifty dollars.

The first time he saw Dave Hanner and Jerry Helluin and Tom Bettis, he told them if they didn't lose twenty pounds each in two weeks, they'd be going home, and they all looked at him like he was crazy. And in two weeks, Jerry Helluin was the only one that didn't lose the weight, and he was gone.

Oh, he had us all afraid of him all right. It wasn't a physical fear. It was a mental thing.

Normally, he didn't bother the defense too much—he let Phil Bengtson handle us—but each week he'd pick out one guy and chew him out, even if he'd played fair. No reason at all, he'd give this one guy hell, and we'd all say, "We'll show that sucker. We'll show him." We were always trying to show him he was wrong. That was his psych, see.

He had all kinds of psychs. During training camp, he'd give everybody hell all day long, and then he'd come around to the rooms at night and chew the fat for five or ten minutes. Every night, he'd pick out a different room—a rookie's, a veteran's, made no difference—and he'd stop in and play a hand of cards or two, or just pat a couple of guys on the head, or say something nice, and then he'd leave. And everybody'd say, "Damn, that man can't be that bad."

Those pep talks of his! I was thirty-six years old, and I thought I had a little sophistication, but when I heard those pep talks, I'd cry and go out and try to kill people. Nobody else could ever do that to me.

I guess the big thing was that he always had something real to say. Nobody else could've gotten away with those pep talks. I know if I tried it today, I'd sound phony as hell. But there was nothing phony about him. Here was a guy that'd gone to church every morning since he was eleven years old, and he believed in everything he said. He had to, because you guys would've seen right through anything phony.

He had his own way of talking. I'd never even thought of "total dedication" in regard to football until I heard him say it. And what was that thing of his: "We all have to have a little love for each other"? I'd never heard that expression used in football, either. "If you don't have it," he'd say, "forget it." No other coach could've used that line without getting laughed at. But he could explain what he meant. "It's not the type of love you have for your wife, your brother, your sister, your mother, your father," he'd say. "It's the type of love you have for your fellow man you work alongside of." And he sure as hell was right.

I'll tell you, I watched Vinny putting that team together, bringing in guys like Willie Davis and Fuzzy

Thurston and Henry Jordan, and getting all you guys to believe in yourselves, and I was sorry as hell I was so old. I would've given anything to be twenty-four again, 'cause I could see what was happening. I could see you guys getting better and better, getting filled with arrogance and proudness, getting to know how good you were. You guys started walking proud. You had to walk proud when you were with him because he walked that way.

During the three years I played out there, I had only one hassle with Vinny. That was during 1960. I was having my best year ever. I'd played every minute of every game, including exhibitions.

We lost our opening game, and then we won three in a row—beat Baltimore and the Lions and San Francisco —and we were getting ready to play Pittsburgh, and *Look* magazine came out to take some pictures for a story. In practice, Gary Knafelc caught a pass off me—caught it out-of-bounds—and Vinny thought I wasn't hustling. "All right, Emlen," he said, "you don't want to play, just get off the field. Get out of here!"

And I walked off the field with tears in my eyes. I just went and got dressed. I was so damn mad, and the rest of the guys were, too, 'cause they had a lot of respect for me. They knew I didn't loaf around.

The next morning, he came in and walked over to my locker and, in front of the whole squad, said, "Emlen, you mad at me?"

"Yeah," I said. "Damn right I am. You acted like a high school coach. Heck, I didn't do anything wrong. The ball was out of bounds. I was hustlin'." I was ready to start crying again.

Vinny stuck out his hand and said, "We still friends?" It took a big man to come to me like that. A helluva big man. He didn't have to do that.

Boy, that was all I ever needed—just a little wink from him, a little kind word, and it made all the work worthwhile.

Outside of that one time, Vinny and I got along fine. I enjoyed playing in Green Bay a whole lot more than I ever expected to. I really liked the guys. They were different. There was no fanfare about them, just regular guys, everybody wanting to play football. I don't know what it was exactly, but I know those were the three greatest years of my life—out there.

All the time I played in Green Bay, I lived in the old Northland Hotel, and people don't know it, but Vinny paid my hotel bill the whole three years. He didn't have to do that, but he did it. It wasn't a lot of money, but it was a lot to me. We didn't get paid so much in those days. We earned our money in Green Bay.

People don't realize a lot of things about Vinny. I remember when we played down in Baltimore in 1961, and my friend Mel Triplett, who'd played with the Giants, showed up at the game. Triplett was drunk as a lord, and the game was sold out, and he didn't have a ticket, but he kept saying he was a friend of Vinny's and mine, and somebody let him into our locker room.

Now, you know the way Vinny felt about the locker room. He never let anyone in there any time, and this was a big game. He looked at Triplett and said, "You keep quiet now, Triplett, and get over there!" And he sat Mel down in a corner of the locker room and sent him over some coffee and let him come out on the field with us, and Triplett got to watch the whole game from the sidelines. Nobody'd ever believe Vinny did things like that.

He did so much for me. When I finally got to the point where I knew, and he knew, I couldn't play anymore, he actually had tears in his eyes. Even before then, he'd given me a job as a scout looking over ballplayers, mostly in the Big Ten, and if it hadn't been for that, I probably would've gotten out of football after I finished playing.

And then last year, he was down at a convention of all the coaches from the black colleges, and somebody asked him if there was anybody around who might be the first black head coach in pro ball, and he said, "Yeah, Tunnell could be a head coach." That made me feel great, 'cause nobody had ever mentioned my name like that.

The last few years at Green Bay, he drove himself so hard that sometimes he'd get sick and pretty near pass out before the games. After he won those three championships in a row, he could've just took it easy the rest of his life. He had all the money and prestige he'd ever need, and I really wondered what he was doing when he went and took the job at Washington. And then I realized that, by his nature, there was just no way he couldn't take the job.

I'm so proud I worked for him and worked with him. You know, a lot of guys try to copy him, but none of them can. All the time I spend around football, I'm always fishing around, looking to find someone like him. But I never have. And I know I never will.

After Emlen and I finished breakfast, I wandered over to the practice field and bumped into Wellington Mara, the president of the Giants. Mara was Vince's classmate at Fordham and one of his chief rivals for academic honors. He had been in frequent touch with Marie, and he knew that Vince's situation was hopeless. "It's so hard to believe," said Mara, whose brother Jack died of cancer a few years ago with similar swiftness. "It's like hearing that the Rock of Gibraltar has a crack in it."

PAUL HORNUNG

"Without Him,
I Don't Know Where I'd Be"

My Green Bay diary began with the following story, and I still know of no better way to capture the special feeling that Vince Lombardi had for Paul Hornung:

On February 10, 1967, I happened to bump into Vince outside the Packer offices, and I greeted him, "Hi, Coach."

He looked at me, and he started to speak, and his jaws moved, but no words came out. He hung his head. Again, he tried to speak, and again he failed.

I could see that he was upset, really shaken. "What is it, Coach?" I said. "What's the matter?"

Finally, Vince managed to say, "I had to put Paul——" He was almost stuttering. "I had to put Paul on that list," he said, "and they took him."

Vince started to walk away. Then he turned. "This is a helluva business sometimes, isn't it?" he said.

Vince had just lost Paul Hornung—to New Orleans in the National Football League's expansion draft. For eight years, ever since Vince came to Green Bay, Paul had been his boy, his protégé, the most vivid symbol of his

*coaching genius. Vince had converted Paul from an un-
happy, uninspired player, typical of the pre-Vince Packers, into a glittering star.*

*Each of Vince's first three years in Green Bay, Paul
led the League in scoring. In 1960, he scored 176 points,
breaking the existing record by almost forty points. Paul
scored his 176 points in a twelve-game season, and even
though the teams began playing a fourteen-game schedule
the following year, no one has come close to his mark. I
suspect it will stand for a long, long time.*

*Paul did everything for us. He ran. He passed. He
caught passes. He place-kicked. He once kicked ninety-
six extra points in a row. He once kicked a fifty-two-yard
field goal. He once scored five touchdowns in a single
game and thirty-three points in another. He was my
favorite football player, and one of my favorite people.
He was Vince's favorite, too.*

*It is a measure of Vince's fairness as a coach that in
1967, when he had to put up one of our running backs
in the draft, he put up Paul, whom he loved, and protected
Elijah Pitts, who was younger and swifter. Vince hated to
lose Paul, but by his own code—"Winning is the only
thing"—he knew that he had no choice.*

*When Paul and I got together in Chicago early in
1970, I asked him about his record-breaking 1960 season.
"How did you manage to score so many points?" I said.*

He blushed. "Just a fantastic athlete, I guess," he said.

*I should have known that Paul wasn't going to tell
the truth—that he owed every point to his fantastic offensive line.*

*Then Paul began to explain how he made Vince
Lombardi into a great coach.*

After that 1958 season, after two frustrating years of
playing quarterback some of the time, fullback some of
the time and halfback some of the time, I just wanted one
thing: To get the hell out of Green Bay. We'd won four
games in two years. We were so bad you married guys

used to hold your parties in the locker room. You didn't want to be seen on the streets.

Then, in the spring of 1959, I heard that we had hired Vince as head coach. Within a few days, I got a phone call from him. It was brief, and to the point, and impressive. "I've been looking at the films," he said, "and you're not playing quarterback anymore. You're my left halfback. You're either gonna play left halfback, or you're not gonna play at all."

I didn't realize it at the time, but that phone call was the start of the eight best years of my life. And Vince was responsible for those eight years, directly responsible. If it hadn't been for him, I couldn't have stuck it out much longer in Green Bay. Till he got there, the whole place was so disorganized that, unless I'd been traded, I would've quit football in a year or two. And even if I'd been traded, I don't think I would have become the football player that Vince made out of me. Without him, I don't know where I'd be today.

If I ever find myself in any kind of difficulty, I know I can turn to him. He's done more for me, on the field and off, than anybody else in my life. When I was suspended from football in 1963 for betting on games, I'm positive he went out on a limb and did everything he could to get me reinstated. Not just because he wanted me back as a football player. He wanted to see me get a second chance. I suppose that was the only time I ever hurt Vince—when I didn't let him know about the trouble I was in, when he had to hear it from the commissioner, from Pete Rozelle, instead of from me.

Vince was the perfect coach for me, the perfect coach for the Green Bay Packers. He taught us what football was all about. I don't believe any team went into its game each Sunday as well prepared as we were. We knew just what to expect, and he knew just how to cope with it.

For instance, if we were playing the Baltimore Colts and we had the ball on the left side of the field between the forty-yard lines, we knew that, on third down, the

Colts would throw up a zone defense against us. And we knew exactly how to attack that zone. The quarterback knew which plays to call, and the linemen knew how to adjust. Every single one of our linemen knew what a zone was. Hell, before Vince got there, even our quarterbacks—I was one of them—didn't know what a zone was. We just called some kind of pass on third down, and that was it. If it went incomplete, we just figured it was a bad pass. We didn't know there was a *reason* it went incomplete.

Vince made us the smartest team in football. Sure, he pounded it into us. He chewed us out. He probably screamed at me more than at anybody else. He had to. For one thing, I was the kind of guy who needed to be pushed. I'd always played under coaches, in high school and at Notre Dame, who yelled at me or slapped me on the helmet or did something to get me going. I expected it, and I wanted it, and Vince knew I never resented it. For another thing, he was showing the other guys on the team that Hornung might be getting all the publicity, but he wasn't getting any preferential treatment. Preferential treatment! Hell, he was all over me. "What's the matter with you, Hornung?" he'd holler. "You got a piano on your back? Can't you run? Move, move, move!" Then, after practice, he'd come over to me and say, "Sometimes I lose my temper and shout at you, but I want you to know it's only for your own good."

He almost killed me for my own good in 1962. I was coming out of the service when I reported to training camp, and I thought I was in pretty good shape. I hadn't worked out much in the Army, but my weight was around 220, pretty close to my playing weight. The only trouble was that I hadn't been running, and my legs weren't in any shape at all. They were so heavy, it was unbelievable. The first two or three weeks in training camp at St. Norbert College, Vince rode me every minute. I don't think he looked at anyone on that field except me. One day, after we finished practice, he made me run ten 100-yard dashes in a row. I thought I was about to die. "You look like you're carrying the whole college on your back!" Vince shouted. That's when you guys started calling me "St. Norbert."

Max McGee was my roommate all through those years, and Max and I had a special relationship with Vince, sort of like a father-son relationship. I don't mean we were so close as father and son, but he would scold us like a father scolding a son. He knew we hadn't committed any mortal sins, that no matter how much trouble we gave him, we were going to keep on playing for him. In a way, we were his favorites. If he hadn't had us to yell at, life probably would've been too dull for him. And we were such good targets, being single and everything.

Vince didn't always understand my sense of humor. You remember the time I was in the Army and I got a weekend pass and played in San Francisco? Before the game, after his speech, Vince went around the team like he always did, asking if anybody had anything they wanted to say. "How 'bout you, Paul?" he said.

"Yeah, Coach," I said. "I've got something to say. I came out to San Francisco for just two reasons. I took care of the first one last night, and now let's go out and beat the 49ers."

Of course, all the guys broke up. Vince probably couldn't understand how everybody could be laughing before a game, but he knew that was one of my roles on the team—to keep us all relaxed. I even loosened him up sometimes.

A lot has been said and written about the times Max and I got into Vince's doghouse, the times he fined us for breaking rules, and some people have gotten the impression we didn't get along with him too well. You know how ridiculous that is. You know how well we got along with Vince. We just had to test him once in a while. Actually, we didn't get fined all that much. He didn't *catch* us every time. I'll admit we did get fined more than anybody else, but, hell, we had more fun than anybody else.

I remember the first time Vince fined Max and me. It

was during his first training camp in 1959. We were all starting to discover what work really was. We were knocked out every day. After lunch, everybody used to jump right in bed just to try to relax their legs for forty minutes. We didn't even have enough strength to find out who was rooming next to us. I think about a hundred different kids came through that camp. He moved them in and out like a herd of cattle. The first few weekends, I was so tired I didn't want to go anywhere but straight to bed. There never was a more quiet dormitory anywhere.

But, you know, after about a month of that Spartan life, you start to go a little buggy. You've got to break out. Vince's rule was that you had to be in bed each night by eleven, with your lights off and your clothes off. One night, Max and I had a couple of dates, and we cut it pretty close coming back. We parked the car in the lot near the dormitory and sprinted straight to our room, and just as we walked in, the eleven o'clock chimes began ringing, and there was Vince, standing in our room, taking bed check. Usually, he let the assistant coaches check the rooms, but there he was that night, right on the stroke of eleven.

"It'll cost you a hundred and fifty each," he said.

"What for?" I said. I had a little courage after a few drinks. "We're in our room."

"You're supposed to be in bed," Vince said. "That's a hundred and a half." And he walked out.

Boy, was I hot! So was Max. "Roomie," I said, "this is very unfair. This is not right. The hell with everything. Let's pack up and go to Miami."

Max agreed with me that Vince had gone too far— Max had tasted a drink or two, too—and by midnight, we were all packed, ready to go. By that time, you and Jimmy Taylor and Bill Quinlan were in our room, watching us.

"Get packed," Quinlan kept saying. "Let's go. Get out of here. You're chicken if you don't go." You were telling us why we shouldn't go, and Max began to weaken, and by that time, you and Jimmy had stolen our luggage and hidden it. Naturally, we couldn't leave—not without our wardrobes. And in the morning, after we'd slept on it, we decided to pay our fines and stick around.

We didn't get caught again until about two years later. Then, on a Saturday night—we had no meetings scheduled the next day—Max and I snuck out of our room after curfew and headed for town. Max finished relaxing about four thirty in the morning and went back to the dormitory. But I decided to sleep out. Around eight thirty or nine, Max called me. "We got caught, roomie," he said. "Vince wants to talk to us."

I didn't believe him. "C'mon," I said. "Cut it out."

"I'm not kidding," Max said. "Vince wants to see both of us together. I'm coming to pick you up."

I thought sure Max was just putting me on. But after he picked me up and started back toward the dorm, he convinced me he was telling the truth. I knew it was going to be some session with Vince. I dreaded it. Forget about the fine. I knew it was going to be a real tongue-lashing.

Vince was in one of the conference rooms downstairs in the dorm, and when we walked in, he was meeting with the coaches. He was standing at the blackboard, writing something, and as soon as he saw us, he got so worked up, the chalk broke in his hand. He started screaming so loud everybody in the dormitory could hear him. I couldn't tell exactly what he was saying at first, but I knew it wasn't complimentary. Finally, he looked at me and hollered, "Hornung! What do you want to be? A playboy or a football player?"

I don't know what got into me. "A playboy," I said.

"Get out of here!" he shouted. "Get out of here!"

He fined us three hundred or five hundred or something like that, and he confined us to quarters for a week. We weren't allowed to leave the dormitory except for meals and practice.

A few years passed before I got Vince that upset again. We were playing in Chicago, and the night before the game, I had a date with a stewardess. We were meeting two other couples for dinner at the Red Carpet, which is one of my favorite restaurants in Chicago. My date and I were the first couple to arrive, and we walked into the bar lounge to have a drink before dinner. There wasn't any waitress working the tables in the lounge right then, and my date looked at the antique bar stools and said, "Let's sit there."

Well, you know, Vince had a rule that we couldn't drink at the bar, at any bar. We could have a drink at a table, but not at a bar. How could I explain that to my date? After all, I was twenty-eight years old. How could I say, "I'm sorry, but I'm not allowed to sit at the bar?"

So we sat at the bar and ordered a couple of martinis. Then I turned to the girl and said, "It'd be something if Lombardi walked in here right now."

"Why?" she asked.

"We're not supposed to sit at a bar," I said.

"Why not?"

"It's just a rule," I said.

I got my martini and took my first sip, and the girl did a double-take and said, "Oh, my God, there's Lombardi!"

I had my back to the foyer, but I knew she had to be putting me on. Still, I turned around, and there he was, with his whole entourage, walking into the bar. I didn't know whether to stand up or hide or what. Finally, I just said, "Hello, Coach."

He exploded. He began ranting and raving at the top of his voice, right in the restaurant. "That'll cost you five hundred," he yelled, "and you're suspended!"

What could I say? How did I know that, of all the places in Chicago, the Red Carpet was one of his favorites, too? My date and I got up and walked out, and in the foyer, the owner of the restaurant, Jerry Kovler, came over to me and said, "Gee, Paul, I'm sorry. I could have told you Vince was coming here. I thought you

VERNON J. BIEVER PHOTOS

As far as the people of Green Bay were concerned, no job was too tough for Vince—except maybe professional golf. He enjoyed the game, but his first love, always, was teaching football.

Vince's moods varied almost as often as his headgear. He and Jimmy Taylor (31) quarreled, and Vince lost Jimmy as a player. But he never lost Jimmy's respect.

With Paul Hornung: A change of pace, Paul talking and Vince listening.

With Ray Nitschke: A helping hand after Vince was knocked down by an opponent's end sweep.

With Bart Starr (left): A few last-minute words of advice.

Fuzzy Thurston: ''Vince put us on the map.''

Henry Jordan: "He treated us all the same—like dogs."

Max McGee: ''Hold on, coach, you're going too fast.''

Frank Gifford (with Bill Austin blocking): "I wanted Vinny to give me a pat on the fanny and let me know I was doing what he wanted me to do."

Jerry Kramer: "Anyone who has spent even a day with him has been better for it."

Willie Davis: "He's all the man there is."

Red Blaik: He spotted something in Vince.

Sam Huff: He came out of retirement for Vince.

knew. Matter of fact, I thought the two of you were probably having dinner together."

Anyway, the next day, I showed up for the game, wondering what Vince was going to do. "I'm starting you," he told me before the kickoff, "but you better have a good game." I did all right, and we beat the Bears, and Vince forgot about suspending me. He even reduced the fine—to three hundred dollars.

There weren't that many incidents—maybe half a dozen in eight years—but there were enough to build up the image of Max and me as the guys who drove Vince wild. Max and I both kind of enjoyed the image, and I think Vince did, too.

One Saturday night last year, after Vince moved down to Washington, Max and I went to see him. We had dinner in a good Italian restaurant with Vince and Marie, and afterward, he invited us back to his house for a nightcap.

Max looked at his watch, and I looked at mine. It was almost eleven o'clock. Max spoke first. "Thanks a lot, Coach," he said, "but we've got to go meet some . . . ah . . . people in a little while."

Vince flashed us that grin of his. "You guys haven't changed at all," he bellowed. "Every senator in this town, every congressman and half the President's cabinet would give anything to spend time with me, and you guys are still running out on me at eleven o'clock!"

Vince was still laughing while Max and I were climbing into a cab and making our getaway.

After I left Paul, I couldn't help thinking about all the years we played together. Paul was really incredible. He loved to have a good time, to party, and I know that if I had tried to follow the social schedule Paul followed, I wouldn't have had the energy to play football. But as hard as Paul socialized, he put as much effort, or more, into football. No matter what he'd done the night before, he'd kill himself on the practice field. He did anything Vince asked him to do. He had complete faith in Vince. Way back in 1959, somebody asked Paul what he thought of Vince, and he said, "If Lombardi told me to move out wide on the next play, jump over the wall, run into the stands and buy a program, I think it would definitely have some direct bearing on the play. It might even score a touchdown."

BART STARR

"I Owe My Life to That Man"

If Paul Hornung was Vince's pet sinner in Green Bay, Bart Starr was his pet saint. In one way, at least, Paul was very jealous of Bart. "When the coaches took bed check," Paul once told me, with something close to awe, "they never checked Bart's room. They knew he was there." Paul always did marvel at perfection.

Paul may have been misused before Vince came to Green Bay, but Bart was practically ignored. He came out of the University of Alabama in 1956 and was drafted during the seventeenth round. The seventeenth-round draft choices who last even one season in the National Football League—Bart has lasted fifteen—are as rare . . . well, almost as rare as Vince Lombardis.

Bart was Green Bay's other quarterback in 1956—behind Tobin Rote.

He was the other quarterback in 1957 and 1958—behind Babe Parilli.

He was the other quarterback in 1959—behind Lamar McHan.

But then, from 1960 through 1969, once the special chemistry clicked between Bart and Vince, Starr was the most successful quarterback in professional football. In individual years, other quarterbacks may have surpassed him—Johnny Unitas, Joe Namath and Sonny Jurgensen

85

*all had brilliant seasons—but for the full decade, no one's
record measured up to Bart's.*

*So many of Bart's accomplishments are remarkable—
he has the highest percentage of completions and the
lowest percentage of interceptions in the history of the
NFL—but there is one that impresses me most. The
average quarterback, in a normal season, has about one
pass in twenty intercepted; the truly exceptional quarterback has about one in thirty intercepted; in six NFL
championship games, against the finest defenses and under
extreme pressure, Bart has thrown 145 passes and has had
only one intercepted.*

*That—like Bart himself—is so good, it's almost unbe-
lievable.*

*Bart and I played golf one day last spring, before we
knew of Vince's illness, and afterward he invited me back
to his home in Green Bay for dinner. There, in his den,
surrounded by mementos of his bright career—he was the
Most Valuable Player in two consecutive Super Bowls and
was named one of the Ten Outstanding Young Men in
the United States in 1969—Bart talked about the coach
who made it all possible.*

I wasn't mentally tough before I met Coach Lombardi.
I hadn't reached the point where I refused to accept second best. I was too nice at times. I don't believe that nice
guys necessarily finish last. I think what Leo Durocher
really meant was that nice guys don't finish first. To
win, you have to have a certain amount of mental toughness. Coach Lombardi gave me that. He taught me that
you must have a flaming desire to win. It's got to dominate all your waking hours. It can't ever wane. It's got to
glow in you all the time.

Coach Lombardi was so demanding and so short on
praise that I would do anything to gain his acceptance,
to get a kind word out of him. I ignored injuries because
he shamed me into it. He would walk into the training
room and see a bunch of guys sitting around getting

treatments, and he'd say, "Who the hell do you think you are? You're not hurting. You're football players." I remember I played an exhibition against Cleveland with a shoulder separation and, I'll admit it, I played lousy. But, jeepers, my shoulder was killing me. And he came up to me during the game and said, "Good God! You're playing like you're crippled!" And I didn't say a word to him about my shoulder because I had too much respect for him. And in 1960, when we had to beat Los Angeles in the final game of the season to clinch the conference title, I was really ill. I got violently sick to my stomach during the game. But I kept playing—I was mentally tough; I wouldn't give in to my sickness—and we won the game.

After that 1960 season—my first as a regular—I went in to discuss my contract with Coach Lombardi. I was probably overfirm trying to compensate for usually being meek and mild in front of him. I made some harsh demands, and he sort of leaned back in his chair and looked at me and said, "My God! I've created a monster!" That just broke me up, and he started to laugh, too.

Of course, I am his creation. I literally owe my life to that man—both on and off the field. People used to say that I was just an extension of Coach Lombardi, a mechanical man who didn't have to think. That didn't bother me. I was proud to be called an extension of him. I wanted to be one of the best quarterbacks in pro football, and I knew I didn't have the strongest arm in the world. I knew I wasn't the biggest guy or the fastest. But Coach Lombardi showed me that, by working hard and using my mind, I could overcome my weaknesses to the point where I could be one of the best. I learned so many things from him that will help me the rest of my life.

Most of all, he gave me self-confidence. Not immediately. When he took the job in Green Bay, one of the first things he did was to acquire Lamar McHan from the St. Louis Cardinals. He felt that he needed a quarterback beyond what he already had, and, naturally, I was a little disappointed because I'd never had a chance to perform for him. It made me feel that he didn't have too much confidence in me.

But as soon as I met him, my disappointment disappeared. He had an early camp for the quarterbacks and the receivers in June, 1959, and his whole approach—the forcefulness of his voice, his carriage, his very presence—oozed confidence. I knew right away that here was a man who was going to take complete charge, who had absolute confidence in his system, and I couldn't wait to see what the system was going to be like.

The heart of his system was preparation. He prepared us beautifully for every game, for every eventuality. That —more than the words of encouragement he occasionally gave me—was what built up my self-confidence. Thanks to Coach Lombardi, I knew—I was positive—that I would never face a situation I wasn't equipped to handle.

Coach Lombardi did a brilliant job of getting us ready for every game we played, but I don't think he ever did a better job than he did preparing us for the National Football League championship game against Dallas in 1966. We had the luxury of two weeks to get ready for that game, and with that much time to study the movies, Coach Lombardi cut all the fat out of our offense. Our game plan for Dallas included eight or ten running plays and about eight passing plays, and that was all—no more than eighteen plays. We had only the plays that Coach Lombardi was positive would work against the Dallas defense, and he was right. We opened the game with a running play to Jimmy Taylor, and that worked, and from then on, every play we tried worked. The game was supposed to be a defensive battle, but it turned into a wide-open offensive game, and we beat the Cowboys, 34–27. [*Bart completed nineteen of twenty-eight passes for 304 yards that game.*]

Basically, I feel, Coach Lombardi is a supersalesman, one of the finest salesmen there's ever been. He has a knack for selling himself and his system and his ideas to football players. He's able to do this because, first, he believes passionately in what he's selling—in himself and his system. And, second, he's a great teacher, both on the field and at the blackboard. For nine seasons, I watched him get up in training camp and diagram his favorite play, the sweep, and talk about it, and I never once got tired of his performance. Every single time, I was captivated.

He would go over every assignment, showing exactly how each man fitted into the play. He would explain how the flanker, whose main assignment was to get the safety, should first try to bump the halfback, to get him off stride. He'd explain how the center and the onside tackle would divide the responsibility for the opposing onside tackle and the middle linebacker. He'd explain how both guards and the offside tackle would pull and how the tight end would handle the outside linebacker and how the onside back would have the key block on the defensive end, and all the time, while he was marking up the blackboard with lines and arrows, he'd be demonstrating blocks, raising his elbows, gritting his teeth, just bursting with enthusiasm. "What we try to do is create an alley," he'd say, and he'd show all the different paths the sweep could follow. "That's the lead play in our offense," he'd say. "We must make it go. We will make it go. We will run it again and again and again, and we will make it go."

The man is a perfectionist, of course, and he was never satisfied simply by a victory. He always wanted us to play as well as we were capable of playing. I don't suppose any of us will ever forget that scene in the dressing room after our exhibition game against the Cardinals in Jacksonville in 1962. Jeepers, we'd just eaten them alive, 41–14, and, still, he chewed the offensive team up and down. Like Fuzzy Thurston said, we thought we were in the Cardinals' dressing room. At the time, most of us thought he was wrong, he was being overly harsh, but when we got home and saw the movies, they bore him out. We had played lousy. The defense had scored all our points, and the offense deserved the criticism he'd given us. He was right, as usual.

I got to know him, really, in the small meetings we'd have every Wednesday, Thursday and Friday mornings. We'd get together around a quarter to nine, just him and the quarterbacks, and it was kind of casual, more like a father and son discussing something they were going to do over the weekend than a lecturer and a listener. He was much more at ease then than he was in front of the whole team.

The better I got to know Coach Lombardi, the more I respected him. I admire what he stands for. He's a high-principled man. He stands for the things I like to think I stand for. They're considered corny in the society in which we live today, because I think there's no longer enough emphasis on loyalty and respect and pride. He stands for self-sacrifice and dedication and religion, and those are values that don't get much attention anymore. But I'll never forget them. He made sure of that.

Coach Lombardi could appear hard-nosed, even vicious at times, the way he talked to us, but, down deep, he respected and loved his ballplayers. I think, more than anything else, he wanted us to be great men after we'd left him, after we'd left football.

The rest of us in Green Bay always felt that, with Bart, Vince was more generous in his praise and more restrained in his criticism than with anyone else. Still, Bart recalls that he would do anything to gain Vince's acceptance. This indicates one of Vince's special strengths: He instilled in us such a burning desire for perfection that, even when he patted us on the back, as he often patted Bart, we weren't satisfied. We still dreaded our next mistake.

As Bart says, he was Vince's creation. All of us were to some degree, but Bart probably more than anyone else. The one year I played in Green Bay before Vince got there, I never noticed Bart. He made no impression on me whatsoever, negatively or positively.

But as the years passed, as other careers faded, Bart became the personification of our team, the personification of Vince's coaching. We all tried to play up to one hundred percent of our ability, and none of us quite made it, but Bart came the closest. Without awesome physical equipment, he made himself the finest football player he could possibly be. That was all Vince asked—that you use your God-given talent to the utmost.

NORB HECKER

"I Would've Worked for Him for Nothing"

The first year Vince coached in Green Bay, he hired four assistants—Phil Bengtson for the overall defense, Norb Hecker for the defensive backfield, Bill Austin for the offensive line and Red Cochran for the offensive backfield—and that staff remained intact through six seasons.

Three of Vince's aides moved up to become head coaches—Austin at Pittsburgh and now at Washington, Hecker at Atlanta and, of course, Bengtson at Green Bay.

Hecker, who played for Los Angeles and Washington during the 1950s, took over the newly formed Atlanta Falcons in 1966 and, in his first season with the expansion team, won three games. The following year, Atlanta won only one game, and when the Falcons got off to a slow start in 1968, Norb was dropped and replaced by Norm Van Brocklin.

Norb, a warm, easygoing man, simply didn't have the players in Atlanta. He did have a most unusual owner, a man named Rankin Smith who, I've heard, once allowed his son, then about eleven years old, to make a draft selection for the team.

Norb is now the defensive coach of the New York Giants and lives in Stamford, Connecticut. I saw him *briefly in the Giants' training camp, when I visited with Emlen Tunnell, and then sat down with him in Connecticut a few days after Vince's funeral.*

Early in 1959, I was back in my home town, Berea, Ohio, wondering what I was going to do for a job. I'd tried playing up in Canada in 1958, but after a few games, my knee had buckled, and I'd spent the rest of the season helping Jim Trimble a little with the coaching.

Then I got a message one night to call Jack Vainisi in Green Bay. Jack was the personnel director of the Packers, but I'd never heard of him. He asked me if I'd fly in to talk to the new coach, Vince Lombardi. I flew there the next day, and Jack picked me up at the airport and drove me to the office to meet Vince for the first time. "I'm looking for a defensive backfield coach," he said.

"Well, I'm looking for a job," I said. "I played eight years of pro ball and I did a little coaching up in Canada."

He never asked me about philosophy or theory of football. He never put me at the blackboard. I found out later he'd gotten some good recommendations about me from coaches I'd played for. He just asked me about my family, my college, my background, all general things, nothing about football.

After about an hour or two, just sizing up my personality, Vince said, "I have to go to New York for a week. I'll call you when I get back."

The next night, he called me from New York. "The job's yours if you want it," he said.

I took it. It was the smartest move I made in my life. The first few years were a learning process for me. Phil Bengtson ran the defense, and he'd say to me, "Do this," or, "Do that," and I'd do it. I was new in coaching, and I was strictly, "Yes, sir." I was just happy to be there. Vince offered me $8,500 to start, and I grabbed it. It was more than I could've made coaching in high school or college. By my seventh year there, I was earning about

$14,000 in salary, which doesn't sound like much now, but I would've worked for him for nothing. You couldn't buy an education like I was getting. What a way to come up as a coach—under a man like that. I never had one salary fight with him. He told me what I'd get each year, and I signed. Sometimes, I didn't have a written contract, just an agreement. Vince was fair. He gave bonuses to all the coaches each year, and we almost always had that nice championship check at the end of the season. You could live pretty will in Green Bay then on the money we were getting.

He was as demanding of the coaches as he was of the players. "I demand the best from all of you," he told us right at the start. "I'm a perfectionist, and there's absolutely no excuse for anything other than that." He'd yell at us, and he'd embarrass us in front of the other coaches, but never in front of the players.

The most he'd say to me in front of the players was like, if somebody caught a pass during practice, "Get on that Whittenton," or "Get on that Adderley." And then I'd tell the guys, "If the old man gets on me, you're gonna catch hell, you can be sure of that" and they'd understand. Once, in 1964, I guess, the year Paul Hornung was having so much trouble with his kicking, and I was the kicking coach, Vince turned to me and said, "Son, if he misses once more, you're fired!" Of course, he didn't mean it. And sometimes, when I had the receiving teams for kickoffs and punts, he'd yell, "Get those guys to catch the ball, Norm. Get on them, Norm!" I coached for him for seven years, and I knew him for twelve, and he never did get my name right. He always called me "Norm," and I always called him, "Coach." Nothing else. I couldn't get up enough nerve to call him "Vince" to his face.

He drove all the coaches, but it never really bothered us because we knew he was working just as hard or harder. The assistants came to work each day around nine o'clock, and he was always in an hour ahead of us. He drove to church every morning—he kept a Bible next

94

to him on the front seat of the car—and then got to the office around eight. Our work weeks during the season were incredible. We'd play a game on Sunday, and then on Monday, we'd watch the films from about nine in the morning till close to midnight, till he got tired. Tuesday, we'd work till about eleven. Wednesday, we'd go from nine to five, then take three hours off for dinner and for him to tape his television show, and then go back for two or three more hours. Our easy day was Thursday; we'd start around nine and finish up around four; that was the only night of the week we could figure on spending at home.

Friday, as soon as practice ended, Red Cochran and Bill Austin and I would take off to scout a college game somewhere. We'd get back to Green Bay or wherever we were playing that week around midnight on Saturday. Sunday night, if we were playing at home, we'd get to see our families again; if we were on the road, we'd get to see an airplane. We once sat down and figured out how much we were making per hour during the season, and we calculated that the garbage men in Green Bay were getting a higher hourly wage.

I remember once, during Christmas week in 1960, we were getting ready to play Philadelphia for the championship, and on Wednesday, Red Cochran went up to Vince and said, "Coach, is there any chance of getting off before nine o'clock tonight? Maybe eight thirty? I could do a little Christmas shopping before the stores close." And Vince pounded the table and said, "Red, you wanna be Santa Claus or you wanna be a football coach? There's no room for both!"

You couldn't argue with Vince about something like that. But you could argue with him about football strategy, and if you were strong enough in your convictions and in your reasoning, you could convince him. There was one way we could always win him over. All we had to do was say, "That's what *you* said yesterday." He had a very short memory in some ways, and if you could make him believe something was his idea, he'd accept it. Of course, it had to be a pretty good idea, or he'd know it wasn't his. I remember when Bill Austin wanted to get a certain play into our game plan, he'd turn to Vince and say, "You said yesterday this would be a good play this week." And Vince'd say, "That's right. Let's put it in."

Phil and I had one little trick we used with him. He hated for us to use a zone defense, because he could always burn a zone himself. He could rip one apart. But once in a while, we put in a safety-up zone; we called it a "Sarah" defense. He'd be watching the movies sometimes and he'd spot something different about our pass defense and, without knowing exactly what, he'd say, "What kind of coverage was that?" And Phil or I would say "That was 'Sarah' coverage, Coach." And he'd say, "Oh, OK." As long as we said "Sarah," it was OK. But if we'd told him it was a safety-up zone, he'd have screamed. He didn't know all the technical aspects of defense. He didn't know the steps and drops and angles, things like that. He didn't have to. He ran the offense and he ran the overall team, and he was a great coach without knowing everything there is to know about defense.

He knew how to delegate authority, and he always had everything so well organized. Everyone had his own assignments, and everyone got his assignments done on time —or ahead of time. Early the first year, he had to say to us a few times, "Where are the game grades? I want 'em on my desk by Thursday noon." But after a while, they were always on his desk Wednesday. Late that year, he got all the coaches together one day, and he said, "You know, we have the makings of a great football team here. In fact, I have the makings of a dynasty." And when he said it, I believed it. I hadn't thought of it before, but I believed him. We all did.

We coaches could always tell Vince's mood when he walked down the hallway in the morning. If I was reading a paper or having a cup of coffee and he passed by and didn't say, "Good morning," I knew what type of day it was going to be. I wasn't going to go in and ask him for anything. I was going to shy away from him all day. I was kind of the middle man between Vince and Dad Braisher, the equipment manager, and when Dad would need a requisition signed, he'd come in to me and say, "Should I ask him today?" And if I'd seen that Vince was in a bad mood, I'd tell Dad to come back the next day. But if Vince was in a good mood, I'd tell Dad to go in, and he'd get that thing signed right away.

Vince sometimes had to get himself into a bad mood whether he really felt it or not. Sometimes we'd watch the movies on Monday and late at night, when we'd finished, he'd say, "I've really got to chew their asses tomorrow. They've really got it coming. I've got to let 'em have it. I know what I'll do. I'll get up early in the morning and have a fight with Marie. Then I'll really bury that ball club. I'll be ready to yell all day."

He'd walk into the coaches' room feeling good some mornings, and he'd say, "Gee, I've got to go in there and chew out this ball club," and then he'd start working himself up to a fever pitch. He'd put on his mad face, get himself angry, and then he'd walk into the meeting room and slam the door as hard as he could, and that was it. He'd start right in on you guys.

I remember one time we played Washington and beat them real bad, but we hadn't played well, at least not in his opinion. He went into the meeting the next day and he started on one guy, I forget who, and he chewed him out, and then went on to the next guy and chewed him out, and then the next guy, straight across the room, and the more he talked, the hotter he got. By the time he got to about the twentieth guy, he was absolutely wild. He had convinced himself and everyone in the room that the team had played a lousy game, and he wasn't going to let anyone get away with that. The coaches felt it, too. He never really gave speeches to just us. We were part of the team, and when he spoke to the players, he was talking to us, too. When he chewed you guys out, he was chewing us out. He could get forty-four men—forty players and four coaches—just by chewing out one man.

The other coaches didn't socialize with him. Maybe Phil did a little, because Phil was his chief assistant and Phil was his age, but the rest of us, we kind of stayed away. He and Phil belonged to the same golf club, but the rest of us belonged to different clubs. We all played golf with him once in a while. He could shoot in the low 80s sometimes, and I could beat him if I got hot, but I never did. No, sir. None of the assistants beat him. If we did, we knew we'd hear how we were spending too much time on the golf course and not enough time on football.

We had a little five o'clock club for the coaches during training camp. We had a room down in the basement of the dormitory, fixed up with a TV and a little kitchen, and all the coaches would go down there for a drink before dinner. We didn't talk football at the five o'clock club unless Vince brought up the subject, and he rarely did. He just wanted to relax and forget about the game for an hour. He'd play cards, but never with anyone else. He'd play solitaire. And he'd watch television, the news shows. He loved to watch the late Senator Dirksen, to listen to him. Vince called him "Mush Mouth." Of course, Vince admired great speakers. He had a record of General MacArthur's famous speech to the cadets at West Point, the one about love and honor and duty, and he used to play that record over and over in the coaches' room. You got tears in your eyes listening to it; it was fantastic.

Vince really loved West Point and Colonel Blaik. He idolized them both. Once, I think it was our second year in Green Bay, he walked into a coaches' meeting and said, "How would you all like to go to West Point and coach?" We all said we'd go with him if he wanted to go. "You won't make much money," he said, "but it's a great life. It's a great place to coach."

I don't think he was completely serious—West Point couldn't afford to pay him anything like what he was worth—but I guess he'd been approached. Blaik had retired the same year Vince came to Green Bay, and his successor hadn't done too well, and I suppose they'd talked to Vince. He must have been tempted.

Vince was beautiful with kids. My wife, Barb, always said that he would have made the greatest Italian Santa Claus. When he laughed, he laughed right up from the bottom of his feet. Many a day, after practice, we'd come off the field, and our wives would be sitting in the stands with Marie, and all our kids would be there. Vince'd come off the field, and about eighteen kids—I had five myself—would run over and grab him around the legs, and he'd pat them and really seem happy. One of our girls, Janie, couldn't pronounce her L's, so she used to call him "Humbuddy." He loved that.

When our fifth child was born, we were living in Green Bay, and we were going to have the christening on a Sunday during the off-season, the Sunday before Easter. Barb invited all the other coaches and she wanted to invite Vince, but she was afraid to. She had some idea that Catholics weren't allowed to go to these things, and she knew how strict a Catholic he was. The day after the christening, I walked into his office and said, "We had our baby christened yesterday"—he was always asking about the kids—and he didn't say much. But the next time he saw Barb, he chewed her out. "You hurt me a little, lady," he said. "You hurt me." Then he told me, "I want you to bring that baby to my house Sunday." It was Easter Sunday, and as far as I was concerned, it was a command performance. I got everybody dressed up and we went over to his new house, and I expected to stay about ten or fifteen minutes. Well, he played with the baby for two hours, on his lap, in his arms, on the floor. I kept looking at Barb and saying, "We've gotta get home and have dinner," and he'd say, "Sit down! The baby's not goin' anyplace." I said, "Yes, sir," and sat down.

I can remember the angriest I ever saw him. We were staying out at the Surfrider Inn in Santa Monica before the last game of the 1960 season. We had to beat the Rams to wrap up the division championship. Phil and

I and Vince had been working all afternoon, and Vince said, "Let's go get something to eat."

"Fine," Phil said.

"Fine," I said. I didn't argue with him about anything.

"Where should we go?" Vince said.

"There's a place right across the street," Phil said.

"Is it all right?" Vince asked.

"Well," said Phil, "it's a place where the players will drink a beer, you know."

"OK," Vince said. "Let's go over there."

It was only about six or seven in the evening, and we walked in, and the bar was on the left and there were a bunch of tables on the right and some booths in the back. You know, he'd always told the players, "If you're drinking, sit at a table. Don't ever let me catch you sitting at a bar." Well, as we came in, there was a group of players at a table, and that didn't bother him, and we walked past, and there was Ray Nitschke, sitting at the bar. "Hi, Coach," Ray said.

Vince was walking in front, with Phil behind him, and me in back, like a little puppy dog. I could see the red starting to come up on Vince's neck. "Let's go back and sit down," he snapped.

We went back to a booth, and they had bowls of peanuts on the tables. We sat down, and as soon as we did, a waiter came over carrying a Scotch and a bourbon and a beer, just what we usually drank. We hadn't ordered anything yet. "Who ordered these drinks?" Vince barked. "We didn't order drinks. Who bought these?"

"That gentleman at the bar," the waiter said, pointing at Nitschke.

And, Jesus, Vince's hand dove into the bowl of peanuts, I'll never forget it, and he started to crunch the shells, and I could see the blood starting to flow, and he got redder and redder. "Let's get out of here," he said. And we got up and walked out. And as we passed the bar, Vince didn't even turn his head. "You're all done," he said, without looking at Ray. "You're through. Get out of town."

We got outside and started to look for another place to eat. We walked down the street, and Phil kept saying, "But we have no other extra linebackers. Nitschke's our only reserve. And we've got to win Sunday. We've got to beat the Rams. We need him."

"He's all through," Vince said. "Get him out of town. He's done. I can't stand that."

We found another place, and all through the meal, Phil kept saying, "We have no other linebackers. What are we gonna do?"

"I don't care," Vince said. "Get rid of him. I don't want him around here."

The more Phil talked, and the more we ate, the more Vince realized we really did need Ray. But he couldn't back down. Finally, he said, "Well, I'll leave it up to the ball club." We knew we had him then. We knew the guys would vote to keep Ray on the club because we needed him. The guys met the next day, and the vote was 39–0, and Ray stayed with the team and, of course, went on to become a great player. But Vince had made his point. He hadn't backed down. He had let the players do it for him.

When Atlanta offered me the head coaching job down there, I went in to talk to Vince about it, and he said, "I already know about it. I talked to Rankin Smith and I know that you're going. Good luck to you. I know you'll do a hell of a job down there."

While I was in Atlanta, I talked with Vince fairly often about possible trades. Even though I was a head coach myself, I still called him "Coach"; he'd always be "Coach" to me. I remember the time I tried to hire Zeke Bratkowski as an assistant. Zeke was ready to quit playing—he was backing up Bart at quarterback—and he wanted to come with me. "I've got to talk to the old man," I told Zeke, "and get the OK from him." I was scared to death to call Vince. Finally, I got up my nerve and phoned him and told him I wanted to hire Zeke, and he almost went through the phone. "Absolutely not!" he screamed.

"Are you kidding? He's a player. He's not gonna coach. I need him." That was in 1967, when Vince was going for that third straight championship.

When I lost my job the following season, the year Vince wasn't coaching, he called me in November and said, "What are your plans?"

"I really don't know," I said. "I'm talking to a couple of teams."

"Well, sit tight," he said. "Don't do anything till I get back in touch with you."

Then, around Christmas, Barb and I went out to Green Bay and I stopped in at the office. "Don't move," he told me. "Don't go anywhere. I've got something going. I'm gonna get back in football, but I can't tell you any more than that now. Keep it to yourself. But I want you with me."

Other teams kept talking to me, and each time I'd call Vince, and he'd say, "Just sit tight. Don't do anything."

Finally, in February, I called him and said, "Can you at least tell me where you're gonna go, so I can look forward to it?" As far as I was concerned, it was all settled, cut and dry, no problem. I was going to go with him.

"It's Washington," he said, "but don't say anything. I'm gonna be in New York next Wednesday. I want you to meet me at the Athletic Club for lunch."

The morning I was meeting Vince for lunch, I went in to see Well Mara, the president of the Giants, and Allie Sherman, the head coach, and they made me a pretty decent offer. Then I met Vince at the New York Athletic Club. We talked about our families for a while, the way we usually did, and then started negotiating. "I'll pay you $20,000," he said.

I probably would've worked for him for $5,000, but I'd learned a little by then, and I felt that he'd give me more if I asked for it. "I've got to have $25,000," I said, "or I can't even consider it." Between $20,000 and $25,000 was the going rate for an assistant coach.

"I've never paid a coach that much," Vince said. "You'd be the highest-paid coach I'm gonna have."

"Well, that's what I've got to have," I said.

"That's a lot of money," he said.

Finally, he gave in, and we shook hands on the deal. "You're my first coach," he said. "You'll have complete command of the defense. We're gonna have a great team. We'll be right back where we were in Green Bay." He was really keyed up, and I was, too. It felt great to be back with the guy, and I could just visualize what was going to happen. With Sonny Jurgensen and all those good receivers, all he needed was some defense, and he'd have a winner.

On our way out of the Athletic Club, I passed Well Mara, who knew I was having lunch with Vince. The next day, I called Allie Sherman and told him I'd made up my mind to go with Vince. "Wait a minute," Allie said. "I'll call you back in fifteen minutes."

In fifteen minutes, Allie was back on the phone. "I just talked to Well," he said, "and this is what we're gonna offer you." And he gave me a figure you wouldn't believe. It probably made me the highest-paid assistant coach in the history of football. It was a helluva lot more money than I'd made as the head coach in Atlanta. I almost dropped the phone. "I'll let you know tomorrow," I told Allie.

Then I called Vince at his home in Green Bay. "Coach," I said, "I've got to talk to you. I'll see you tomorrow morning in Green Bay." And I hung up and got ready to leave for Wisconsin.

I walked into his office in the morning, shaking like a leaf, I was so nervous. "I know we made an agreement," I said, "but let me tell you what happened . . ." And then I told him about the figure the Giants had offered me, and Vince said, "I don't believe it. I knew that Mara would do that to me."

We talked for a while. We talked about my responsibility to my family, about how much I wanted to go with him. "I've got to have some security," I said. "If you'd only give me a three-year contract . . ."

Vince never fired a coach as far as I know, but he just didn't believe in more than one-year contracts. "You don't need a contract," he told me. "As long as I've got a job, as long as I'm in football, you've got a job."

"I know, Coach," I said. "I know that. But what if something should happen to you? I've got a family, and God forbid anything should happen to you, I'm out looking for a job."

I had the feeling that he wanted to coach the Redskins just for three or four seasons, then step down and concentrate on being an owner.

"What would you do?" I said. "How can I pass up this offer from the Giants?"

"I don't see how you can afford not to take it," he said. "Forget about our handshake. There's no ill feelings. You're a good coach, and you shouldn't turn down that offer. It wouldn't be fair to your family. Good luck there."

Vince was letting me off the hook, and I felt miserable. The Giants had offered me a multi-year contract at more money than I'd ever expected and, honestly, if he'd just given me a three-year contract and $25,000, I wouldn't have hesitated. I'd have gone with him. That was how much I thought of him.

After we had talked for hours about the bright days in Green Bay, the days when we both feared and loved Vince, Norb and I talked about the funeral. "At the church," Norb said, "I looked at the coffin, and I said, 'He's not in there. That's an empty coffin.' There was no way I could visualize him being in that coffin. If anyone was going to live forever, he's the guy.

"He'll never be dead in my mind. To me, he's still coaching. Still the coach. I can still see him, out there in that T-shirt and those baggy khaki pants, like knickers, with that whistle around his neck and the sunglasses and baseball cap on. I just don't believe he's no longer here."

I had a similar feeling. I won't accept the fact that

Vince is gone, either. At the cemetery in New Jersey, I stood close to the coffin and kept waiting for something to happen. Now he's gonna come out, *I was thinking.* Enough of this. *I waited and waited, and the short ceremony ended, and the family got up and left, and some guy next to me was clicking away with a camera, and I wanted to chew his head off, and all the people began to leave, and I waited, waited for something to happen, waited for someone to tell me that the joke was over.*

Soon, some workmen came, and they put some dirty, ugly, rusty hooks on the four corners of the coffin, and they started to lower it into the ground. They got about halfway through, and I turned away. I couldn't watch it go down. I walked away. To me, he'll never be gone or buried.

And as I left the cemetery, I noticed a cluster of young children, drawn by the ceremony and by the visitors, and I couldn't help wondering who would teach them the importance of sacrifice and of self-discipline and of loyalty and of dedication. Who would be their Vince Lombardi?

WILLIE DAVIS

"He Made Me Feel Important"

By the end of 1959, his first season in Green Bay, Vince had hit upon the offensive lineup that was going to win National Football League championships in 1961 and 1962. Still, the defense wasn't set, and in 1960, he picked up two unheralded, but key men: Willie Wood came to us as a free agent, fresh from the University of Southern California, and Willie Davis came to us from the Cleveland Browns, where he had been an understudy for a couple of seasons.

When I first saw Willie Davis, with his big torso and his relatively slender legs—his "getaway sticks," we called them—I was skeptical about his reputation for speed. I challenged him to a race. We both got down in three-point stances, and someone yelled, "Go," and he jumped and just beat me. We did it again, and I jumped and just beat him. That was enough for me; I didn't race Willie anymore.

Willie broke into our starting lineup right away, and by 1962, he was an All-Pro defensive end. Willie made All-Pro five out of six years and, in 1966, became captain of our defensive team, by then the toughest defensive unit in pro football.

In 1968, my final season, Willie and I were roommates. We were among the handful of starters remaining from

Vince's first championship team, and whenever we stopped and realized that Vince and Paul Hornung and Max McGee and Jimmy Taylor and Fuzzy Thurston were up in the stands, watching us play, we felt old and tired and out of place.

Willie stayed on one year longer than I did, then retired and moved to Los Angeles. He had spent several off-seasons working for the Schlitz Brewery people, and in 1970 he purchased his own Schlitz distributorship in Los Angeles. We met there in February, not long after he launched his new career, and we polished off a few of his products and talked about Vince, who was then cheerfully looking forward to his second season with the Washington Redskins.

When I heard in 1960 that I'd been traded to Green Bay, I was really disappointed. You know, Paul Brown, our coach in Cleveland, was always threatening us that if we didn't play well, he'd send us to Green Bay.

If, when I showed up in Green Bay, Vince had said something to me like he wasn't sure whether or not I could do the job, I probably would've just given up on the National Football League and gone to Canada to play.

But Vince was in my corner right away. "We think you can help us," he said, "and we're going to give you a chance to show us what you can do." He asked me about my contract, and I dropped my head about the small amount I was getting from the Browns, and Vince said, "Well, we're giving you a thousand more to start." He made me feel like I was wanted. He made me feel important.

I was ready to play football. You remember what I always liked to say: Vince came to Green Bay and turned the team around, and then I came and took 'em in the right direction.

Football is a game of emotion, and what the old man excels at is motivation. I maintain that there are two driving forces in football, and one is anger, and the other is fear, and he capitalized on both of them. Either he got us so mad we wanted to prove something to him or we were fearful of being singled out as the one guy who didn't do the job.

In the first place, he worked so hard that I always felt the old man was really putting more into the game on a day-to-day basis than I was. I felt obligated to put something extra into it on Sunday; I had to, just to be even with him.

Another thing was the way he made you a believer. He told you what the other team was going to do, and he told you what you had to do to beat them, and invariably he was right. He made us believe that all we had to do was follow his theories on how to get ready for each game and we'd win.

I knew we were going to win every game we played. Even if we were behind by two touchdowns in the fourth quarter, I just believed that somehow we were going to pull it out. I didn't know exactly how or when, but I knew that sooner or later, we'd get the break we needed —the interception or the fumble or something. And the more important it was for us to win, the more certain I was we would win.

That whole feeling disappeared in one game in 1968, the first year he wasn't coaching us. We had to beat the 49ers out in San Francisco. We had a thirteen-point lead going into the final quarter, and we knew that Minnesota had already gotten beat by Los Angeles. As long as we could hold onto our lead, we'd move into first place. And we lost. That ended the string. That ended the philosophy. That was the last time I went into a game believing that, no matter what happened, we were going to win.

Probably the best job I can remember of him motivating us was when we played the Los Angeles Rams the next-to-last game of 1967. We had already clinched our divisional title, and the game didn't mean anything to us, and he was worried about us just going through the motions. He was on us all week, and in the locker room before the game, he was trembling like a leaf. I could see his legs shaking. "I wish I didn't have to ask you boys to go out there today and do the job," he said. "I wish I could go out and do it myself. Boy, this is one game I'd really like to be playing in. This is a game that you're playing for your pride." He went on like that and he got me so worked up that if he hadn't opened that locker-room door quick, I was going to make a hole in it, I was so eager.

And we played a helluva game. We had nothing to gain, and the Rams were fighting for their lives, and they just did manage to beat us. They won by three points when they blocked a punt right near the end.

Then, you remember, a couple of weeks later, we played Los Angeles again for the Western championship of the NFL, and he had us all feeling that we weren't going out to win for the Green Bay Packers, but to preserve our manhood. I don't recall his exact words, but it was something like this: "If you don't beat these guys this time, you're going to have to live with it the rest of your lives. If these guys can come into your own backyard and whip you, after they beat you out on the Coast, they'll think they can beat you anywhere, on a street, in an alley, on the corner of Sunset and Vine. You'll have to run from those guys for the rest of your lives." He got to me. If I let those guys beat me, I'd never be able to face them again. I'd never be able to face myself again. And we went out and played great football and we whipped them good and preserved our manhood.

There were so many things he could do to get you fired up. Maybe we'd been playing good and starting to feel satisfied with ourselves, and he'd get us together and say, "You owe something to these people who are coming out to see you today. When this game ends, I want them to say they just saw the greatest team they ever saw. They just saw the greatest defensive end they ever saw. They just saw the greatest offensive guard they ever saw. If they don't come out saying that, your record doesn't mean anything. They're going to think yesterday was a fluke. You've got to prove yourself all over again."

You never could predict how he was going to act. The days you really expected him to go through the ceiling, he'd come in and be very soft. He'd say something like, "You're a better football team than you showed today." Or he'd blame himself and the other coaches for not preparing us properly. He'd never let us slip into a defeatist attitude. But then sometimes, when you figured you'd played pretty decent—maybe you'd lived up to what you thought he expected of you—he'd come in and drop the bomb on you. Like one time we beat Minnesota, and didn't play all that bad even though they scored a lot of points, and he walked into the locker room and said, "I'd like our front four to apologize to the rest of the team. You cheated on us today. You should apologize. You didn't play the kind of football you're capable of playing." His words kind of froze me. I felt awful.

One time, when we thought we'd played a good game, he started in on us, "Who the hell do you think you are? The Green Bay Packers? The Green Bay Nothings, that's who you are. You're only a good football team when you play well together. Individually, none of you could make up a team. You'd be nothing without me. I made you, mister."

How about the day we beat the Rams, 6–3, in Milwaukee in 1965? We'd broken a two-game losing streak, and we were all kind of happy and clowning around, and he came in and you saw his face and you knew nothing was funny anymore. He kicked a bench and hurt his foot, and he had to take something out on somebody, so he started challenging us. "Nobody wants to pay the price," he said. "I'm the only one here that's willing to pay the price. You guys don't care. You don't want to win."

We were stunned. Nobody knew what to do, and, finally, Forrest Gregg stood up and said, "My God, I want to win," and then somebody else said, "Yeah, I want to win," and pretty soon there were forty guys

110

standing, all of us shouting. "I want to win." If we had played any football team in the world during the next two hours, we'd have beaten them by ten touchdowns. The old man had us feeling so ashamed and angry. That was his greatest asset: His ability to motivate people.

He never got me too upset personally. Of course, I had pretty thick skin by the time I got to Green Bay. Paul Brown had chewed on me so much in Cleveland that when I got to the Packers, Vince was a welcome sight. Vince and Paul Brown were similar in the way they could cut you with words and make you want to rise up to prove something to them.

I think Vince got on me sharp maybe twice in eight years. I remember once, after the Colts had been hooking me on the sweep, he ate me up, and Max McGee said, "Well, I've seen everything: Vince got on Willie Davis."

Maybe he wasn't as tough on me as he was on some people, but, I'll tell you, I hated to have him tell me I was fat. I hated to have him tell me I didn't have the desire anymore. He'd just say those things to the whole team—"You're all fat; you don't want to win anymore"—and I'd get so angry I couldn't wait till I got out on the field.

I guess maybe my worst days in football were the days I tried to negotiate my contracts with the old man. I'd get myself all worked up before I went in to see him. I'd drive up from my home in Chicago, and all the way, I'd keep building up my anger, telling myself I was going to draw a hard line and get just as much money as I deserved.

One year, I walked into his office feeling cocky, you know, "Roll out the cash, Jack, I got no time for small change." All he had to do was say one harsh word, and I was really going to let him have it. I never got a word in. Soon as he saw me, he jumped up and began hugging me and patting me and telling me, "Willie, Willie, Willie, it's so great to see you. You're the best trade I ever made. You're a leader. We couldn't have won without you, Willie. You had a beautiful year. And, Willie, I need your help. You see, I've got this budget problem . . ."

He got me so off-balance, I started feeling sorry for him. He had me thinking, "Yeah, he's right, he's gotta save some money for the Kramers and the Greggs and the Jordans," and the next thing I knew, I was saying, "Yes, sir, that's fine with me," and I ended up signing for about half what I was going to demand. When I got out of that office and started driving back to Chicago, I was so mad at myself, I was about to drive off the highway.

The next year, finally, I got him. I went into his office and I said, "Coach, you're quite a guy. I got to be very frank, Coach, I just can't argue with you. You know, you just overwhelm me. So I've jotted down a few things I want to tell you." And I handed him a letter I'd written.

He started reading the letter—and I'd put a lot of stuff in it, like how I felt about the fans and what he'd done for me and how many years I had left—and, at first, he gave me that "heh . . . heh . . . heh" of his. Then, when he got around to how much money I wanted, he put his frown on me. He looked at me and said, "I can't argue with what you say here, Willie, but I can't pay you that much money."

"Well, Coach," I said, "I really feel that way."

He thought it over a little and said, "I'll tell you what I'll give you," and named a figure not too much below what I was willing to settle for. "You'd be one of the highest-paid linemen in the whole league," he whispered, like he was afraid somebody might hear him.

"Look, Coach," I said, "I really thought hard about this, and I got to have a thousand dollars more than that. It's only a thousand dollars, but it's the difference between me driving back to Chicago today feeling real good and driving back to Chicago wanting to go head-on into somebody. It's really what I feel like I'm worth."

"If it's that important to you," he said, "you got it."

I felt good. I had my letter in my hand and I started to

walk out, and he said, "Hey, wait a minute. Let me have that letter. Let me keep it. I don't want you giving it to anybody else."

When I took over the distributorship out here, I called my salesmen together and gave them a little speech. "I don't care who's out there," I said. "I don't care who you're competing with. You're going to do better than them. You're not going to be second-best. You're going to go after them. When you walk into an account, I want you to be prepared to sell that man. I want you to make him feel you're the most important salesman that walks in his door. I want you to let him know how you're going to help him. You're going to help make him a success, and you're going to be a success." The speech went on like that, and when it was over, all my salesmen came to me individually and told me it was the greatest sales talk they'd ever heard. It should've been. I took every single thought from Vince.

Willie's doing great in the beer business. The sales in his area are way up over the year before, something like a quarter of a million cases, he told me.

It's ironic, but because of Vince, Willie almost didn't go into the distributorship. In 1968, when Vince was negotiating with the Washington Redskins, he told Willie, "I'm taking you with me." He wanted to take Willie and Forrest Gregg with him as assistant coaches, but Pete Rozelle, the commissioner of the National Football League, told Vince when he accepted the job with the Redskins that he couldn't bring along anyone from Green Bay.

If the commissioner hadn't made that ruling, my old roommate might be a football coach now, instead of a beer baron.

When Vince died, Willie offered one of the most moving epitaphs. Somebody asked him how he felt about Vince Lombardi, and Willie said, summing everything up in one simple sentence, "He's all the man there is."

HENRY JORDAN

"He Didn't Push; He Led"

Before his first season in Green Bay, Vince acquired two defensive linemen from the Cleveland Browns—Bill Quinlan, an end, and Henry Jordan, a tackle. Henry cost Vince only a fourth-round draft choice, yet starting in 1960, for five straight years, Henry was an All-Pro defensive tackle.

He was also one of the most popular after-dinner speakers in Wisconsin. A Virginian, with an easy drawl and an easy manner, Henry entertained his audiences with dozens of stories, and a large percentage of them were about Vince. It was Henry who coined what may be the most quoted line about Vince: "He treats us all the same —like dogs." And it was Henry who said, "When he tells you to sit down, you don't look for a chair."

Henry swears that his favorite Lombardi story is a true one. "One morning," he says, "we went out to the stadium, and it was pouring down rain. I just took one look at the sky and I knew it was gonna rain all day. We had a longer meeting than usual, figuring we'd never got out to the field to practice, and Lombardi was pretty unhappy, walking around, wringing his hands, looking disgusted with the weather.

"Finally, he cut out pacing and looked up at the heavens and shouted, 'Stop raining! Stop raining!' And *there was a huge clap of thunder and a flash of lightning, and the rain stopped.*

"I'm a hard-shelled Methodist, but I've been eating fish every Friday since then."

Henry retired from the Packers after the 1969 season and took a fulltime job as executive director of the Summerfest, a ten-day entertainment spectacular held in Milwaukee every July. In the spring of 1970, I stopped by his home—he lived directly across the street from me during most of the years we played together—to chat about Vince. "You know," Henry said, "when he left here, it cost me forty-five minutes of my speech."

I'd already been in camp with the Browns for five weeks in 1959 when I got traded to Green Bay. I'd showed up for camp weighing 265 pounds, and I'd dieted and worked hard and, in five weeks, I'd lost fifteen pounds. The first thing I noticed when I got here was that there weren't too many big boys around. We had a few 270-pounders in Cleveland, but the biggest one here was Dave Hanner, and he was just over 260. "Why, this is nothing but a bunch of little boys," I said. Then I found out why. After three days in Lombardi's training camp, I was down to 235.

Paul Brown's philosophy in Cleveland was that you got yourself in shape; he didn't put much emphasis on conditioning. Lombardi, on the other hand, ran you and ran you and ran you, but I don't think it was so much for conditioning as for discipline. He figured that, after we finished practice, we'd all be too tired to be cliquish or clannish or give him any trouble.

I was fortunate to play under two of the best coaches in history, and each had his own way, and each's way worked for him. Paul Brown was very detailed in what he wanted you to do; when you lined up, for instance, you knew exactly which foot he wanted back and how he wanted you to step off. Lombardi didn't do that; he'd tell you what he wanted accomplished, and then he'd let

115

you do it any way you wanted as long as you got the job done.

The fundamental difference between them was that Lombardi would talk to you man-to-man, and Paul Brown would talk to you from a pedestal. Lombardi would call you a dummy and dare you to swing at him, and if you ever did, you knew he'd swing back. Paul Brown would put himself above you and talk down to you, and there was never any question of anybody swinging at anybody.

Lombardi's approach was man-to-man, but I don't mean it was friend-to-friend. It was always coach-to-player. I don't think I ever really knew Lombardi as an individual, as a person, because he would never let himself relax with us. He couldn't. He had forty powerful, egotistical animals to control, all strong physically, all strong-willed and all big shots where they came from. Suddenly, they found themselves with thirty-nine other guys just as strong, and one man leading them, and if Lombardi had let down one inch, they'd have taken advantage of him.

He never let down, and I can't argue with his methods, because he got the utmost out of each one of us. Individually, I don't think we were a match for several other teams, but, combined, we beat them. For example, you put me in there alone with Merlin Olsen, and he'd take me and crunch me; Merlin used to introduce me to people as his dad. And you take Willie Davis and put him up against Deacon Jones, and you had to figure Deacon would destroy him. But you put Willie and me together, and we did just as well for Green Bay as Merlin and Deacon did for Los Angeles. Why? I guess because we thought we could—we knew we could. And maybe after going through a week with Lombardi, we were more afraid of him than of any other team.

I always respected Lombardi, and one of the things I liked best about him was that he made us all feel part of the team. I can remember him coming up to me and saying, "Henry"—he called me "Henry" sometimes and "Bob" sometimes and "Dave" sometimes and "No. 74" sometimes; I was sort of an unknown—"Henry, I want you to play this play normal and tell me what you think about it." And then he'd have you guys run a new play, and I'd tell him exactly what I thought of it, why I thought it'd work or why I thought it wouldn't. This little technique of his worked two ways: First, he got the opinion of a veteran who'd been up against similar plays for a number of years and, second, he made me feel a part of everything. He did this with all the guys. He knew what he was doing; he was an intelligent man.

A lot of people have said that Lombardi pushed us, but I've been thinking about that, and it's not really true. He didn't push; he led. He didn't force us to do anything he wouldn't do himself. Take the time he bought that weight machine for us. He told us he wanted us to go in there and lift 250 pounds every day. He was in there every day, too. Maybe he'd only lift twenty-five pounds, but he'd be in there. He showed us he believed in it, for himself as well as for us. I think every coach ought to be like that. If he wants you to do thirty minutes of calisthenics, well, he better do five minutes himself. He better be a leader, if he wants to be a winner.

I may be unusual, but I don't think Lombardi ever really motivated me, ever got me to play over my head or anything like that. I didn't need anyone to motivate me. Ever since I was twelve years old, I've been driven by some kind of need to be a success. Some guys need praise, and some guys need chewing out, but I don't think I needed anything. Still, he used to abuse me a lot. Maybe he thought he was motivating me—even though I didn't— but I think that was only his secondary purpose. I think he was using me to motivate some of the other guys, particularly the younger fellows. Maybe some of them needed a chewing out, but if Lombardi had just chewed them out, they'd have thought they were being picked on. As long as Lombardi chewed me out first, they couldn't figure that way. He used you like that, too. I guess it helped the team, but it didn't help me much. His yelling didn't motivate me. It just made me mad.

Some of his yelling, I couldn't take too seriously. For instance, he used to holler at us, "You couldn't earn $6,000 a year outside of football." He yelled that at me for nine years, and it was just plain ridiculous. I earned $6,000 a year when I was in high school. Another thing he used to shout was, "OK, you don't want to play here, I'll give you a release. Go someplace else. You won't be any good anywhere else."

Well, I tested him on that in training camp in 1967. We were working out, and he was screaming at everybody, "You gotta lose some weight, you gotta lose some weight." And he looked at me, and I don't think he looked very close, and he said, "You, too, Henry, you're a disgrace."

I felt I was in good shape. I'd reported to camp at 257 pounds, right where I wanted to be. I knew I'd end up opening the season around 243 or 245. But when he said, "Lose some weight," I said, "OK, I'll show him." I just quit eating. In four days, I went down to 246. Then we had a scrimmage, and it was a miserably hot day, and you can imagine how weak I was, not having eaten in four days. I wasn't trying to impress anybody in that scrimmage. I was just trying to survive. Then we watched the films and, of course, I looked terrible, and he started chewing me out, which I expected. But once he got his teeth into me, he wouldn't let go. He got into me for about fifteen minutes, you know, the usual sort of stuff, "You're a disgrace and you ought to be ashamed of yourself and if you don't want to play here, get the hell out, I'll give you your release."

I turned in my play book. I quit. I told him, "OK, give me my release." I was serious. I knew there were a lot of teams looking for a defensive tackle with a little experience, and I knew they'd pay me twice what I was getting.

"You unhappy with your money?" he said.

"No," I said, and that kind of surprised him, because he thought I was just looking for more money.

"Well, what do you want?" he said.

118

"I want to be released," I said. "You said I could be released and go someplace else, and that's what I want."

"You've got to be kidding," Lombardi said. "You're not going anyplace else. You're gonna live and die right here."

And, sure enough, we made up, and that's what happened.

He was a tough man with money, but I remember one training camp, when I hadn't signed my contract and I was working out, I went to him and said, "Coach, I need an advance. My wife's in the hospital, and I need some cash."

"Fine," he said. "You go see Ruth"—she was the Packers' accountant—"and tell her what you need and she'll write you a check."

I thanked him and then, as I started to walk off, he said, "And while you're there, sign your contract."

"Now, wait a minute," I said. I thought he was trying to slip something past me.

"Sign your contract," he repeated. "If you don't sign today, you're not going to get . . ." And he named a figure, which was more than a thousand dollars more than I was asking for, and I hurried and went and signed before he changed his mind.

He had a real feeling for the family: Take care of your family first, he said, and he meant it. Once, when my little boy Butch broke his leg, I was down at the hospital, and a nurse came over to me and said there was a phone call for me. I picked up the phone, and a voice said, "Henry, this is the coach."

"Coach who?" I said.

"Coach Lombardi," he said. "How's your son?"

I was flabbergasted. I never expected him to call.

And way back in my first season, when my wife's mother was killed in a car accident and I had to fly home for the funeral, the Packers paid my way and sent the biggest wreath of flowers there was at the funeral. I never forgot that.

I don't think I'd want to be like Lombardi. I think it

takes too much out of you. You drive like that, you've got to give up a lot of time with your family, and you lose a lot physically. I remember he told me once, just before he stopped coaching us, "This job is getting to me, Henry. I have to take a nap every afternoon."

Still, now that I'm in business, I'm applying Lombardi's principles. I sent my secretary home crying my first three days on the job. One gal retired on me. I was putting them through training camp. I walked in and the first thing I said was, "Your job is on the line. If you don't make it, you're out, you're through."

I said to the secretary, "What the heck you been doing all day? I don't see anything you've done." And if she gave me a letter and there was one mistake in it, I'd make a big X all the way across it and say, "Type it again." It worked out pretty well. They're organized now. I don't have the slightest idea of what they think of me, but they're working. I don't cuss or raise my voice, but I'm strict. A lot of him has rubbed off on me.

But there's one big difference. I want to relax and enjoy life; that's my idea of happiness. To Lombardi, happiness was only one thing: Lying exhausted in victory.

Olive Jordan, Henry's wife, sat in on our conversation, and when I asked Henry if he felt Vince was compassionate, Olive volunteered her opinion. "From my standpoint," she said, "he had a lot of compassion—toward a wife, a family, children. One time I went shopping with my daughter Suzanne, who was then an infant, and a babysitter. I was driving an old car we had, and I left Suzanne and the babysitter in the car when I ran into the store. When I came out, the babysitter told me that Suzanne had been at the window, smiling and waving at everyone, and a man had come down the street and waved back and walked up to the window and smiled at Suzanne. And the babysitter almost fainted because the man was Lombardi. He didn't recognize the car, because it wasn't Henry's, and he didn't recognize Suzanne, because he couldn't know all the players' children, and, of course, he didn't recognize the babysitter. But he had compassion for a little baby waving to him, and he wanted to make sure that he didn't hurt her feelings."

Olive mentioned that once, when she was pregnant during training camp, she drove to the dormitory one afternoon to pick up Henry. "I walked in the front door," she said, "and Lombardi was standing there, and he saw that I was very, very heavy with child and he put his arms around me and gave me a big hug and a smile and said, 'Isn't that wonderful?' It surprised me. He was so rough with the men, and a lot of times Henry would come home and he'd be so angry, and I'd wonder just what kind of a man Lombardi was. I always felt that he didn't quite know how to act around the wives, because he knew what our husbands must be saying to us about him. But if you were friendly and outgoing with him, then he'd relax. He seemed to be thinking, Well, fine, you're not holding it against me, 'cause I'm just doing my job, and I expect your husband to do his."

At that point, Henry interrupted. "Besides," he said, "as soon as he saw you were pregnant, Lombardi figured he had me again. Easy signing at the contract table. Wife's pregnant. That takes care of Henry for this year."

DON CHANDLER

"He Controlled His Emotions"

Donny Chandler played twelve seasons in the National Football League, his first three under Vince in New York and his last three under Vince in Green Bay. If anyone followed Vince's code—"Winning is the only thing"—it was Don. Nine times in twelve years, the team he played on won its divisional championship. Don is one of only two men to have played in nine NFL title games; the other, Lou Groza, spread his appearances over seventeen seasons.

Don joined us in Green Bay in 1965 and led us in scoring each year as we won three straight NFL championships and the first two Super Bowls. His final season was his best. He made nineteen of twenty-six field goal attempts, thirty-nine of thirty-nine extra point attempts, then finished with a flourish, a Super Bowl record of fifteen points, including four field goals in four tries.

He retired after the Super Bowl, and we missed him badly in 1968. Our field goal production slipped from nineteen for twenty-six to thirteen for twenty-eight (I missed five of nine). Six additional field goals in exactly the right places would have changed our record from 6–7–1 and third place to 10–4 and the divisional championship. It was just too much for us to lose, in a single season, both Vince's mind and Donny's toe.

DON CHANDLER

Don and I have been partners, since our retirement from football, in real-estate investments in his home town, Tulsa, and during one of my trips to Oklahoma early in 1970, we sat down and swapped impressions of Vince.

My rookie year in pro football, 1956, was almost my last year in pro football. Sam Huff and I played in the College All-Star game, then reported to the Giants in Winooski, Vermont. We played an exhibition in Boston, and afterward we took a train back to Vermont and got right off the train and started practicing. I had a bad shoulder and Sam had a bad knee, and Lombardi was all over us. As far as he was concerned, we couldn't do anything right.

We decided we were going to quit. Sam felt he wasn't big enough to make it in pro ball, and I felt I wasn't good enough, and it just wasn't worth putting up with all his hollering.

When we went to hand in our play books, we couldn't find any coaches around. Finally, we went to Lombardi's room, and he was in his bed, asleep. We walked in and threw our books down on his desk and said, "We quit," and just as we did this, he woke up. He bolted out of his bed and came after us. I took off, running as fast as I could, but Sam's knee was hurting and he couldn't run. I got out of the dadgummed dormitory, but he had Sam cornered. I could hear him yelling, "You might not make this team, but you're sure as hell not gonna walk out on us!"

Lombardi wouldn't let Sam go, but I grabbed hold of one of the other rookies and talked him into taking me to the airport. He was glad to do it; he was trying out for running back, just like I was.

The head coach, Jim Lee Howell, chased out to the airport and got me to come back. The next day, incidentally, the kid who'd given me the ride got cut from the squad.

I went back and stuck it out, but Lombardi never did let up on me. "You're running in mud," he'd yell. "You run like you got a board in your back." He had something to say all the time.

One day in practice, he called a 49-option, the option pass, and my shoulder was so bad I couldn't throw a football. But, instead of telling him that, I went through with the play and ran with the ball. Of course, he wanted me to try a pass, so he called the same play again, and again, instead of throwing, I ran. He started chewing me out something terrible, calling me names and everything, and I yelled back at him. I remember I said, "Rome wasn't built in a day," and a few other things, and then somebody told him about my shoulder and he didn't say anything more to me.

I think he kind of respected me for shouting back at him, but to be honest, we never did get along worth a damn in New York. In the first place, since I was a running back, I was one of his boys, one of his responsibilities, so he felt he had to holler at me. And in the second place, I was a second-string running back, behind Frank Gifford and Alex Webster and Mel Triplett, and you know how he always was: Tough on the first stringer, but double tough on the guy behind him.

My first three years in New York, when he was coaching the offense, I got to run with the ball occasionally, but mostly I just handled the punting. A few years after Lombardi left New York, Pat Summerall retired, and I became the regular place-kicker for the Giants. By the time Lombardi traded for me in 1965, I'd long forgotten about being a running back. I was strictly a punter and placekicker.

Our relationship was entirely different in Green Bay. As soon as he got me, he called me up to New York—not Green Bay—to sign my contract, and he sat down with me and went over the whole team, the offense and the defense, telling me the strengths and weaknesses, the changes he was planning, the problems he'd had in 1964. That was the year you were out, and Paul Hornung wasn't kicking well, and he felt that if he'd had a good kicking game, he'd have won the championship. I guess he felt that I was a part of his past and, therefore, he could confide in me. Besides, I didn't know the guys, and I wasn't the kind who was going to repeat what he told me. He wasn't looking for my advice or anything. He just wanted someone to talk to.

He left me pretty much alone as a place-kicker and punter. I don't mean entirely. I remember one day we were having punt-return practice, and the worst thing to do to a punter is to make him kick for punt returns. I don't know why, but there's no way you can kick right in that kind of practice. Donny Anderson and I were alternating punts, and I was kicking badly, and he started hollering at me. "If you can't do any better than that," he said, "we'll get somebody else."

"Well, you better get somebody else then," I said.

I guess I snapped back at him so quick because I'd gotten out of the habit of being yelled at. Then I went into the locker room, and I just sat there, not knowing what the hell was going to happen. If he'd come in screaming, I don't know what I would've said. But he walked in kind of jauntily and came over to me and said, "You know, you're kicking too much. You ought to lay off a little. Relax a bit." He knew he'd pushed me far enough.

He knew how to pick me up, too. In 1966, I had what I thought was a miserable year. The year before, I'd made about two-thirds of my field goal attempts, but in 1966, I didn't even make half. I was totally unhappy with myself, and I made a special trip up to Green Bay during the off-season to talk to him. I wasn't sure about coming back in 1967. I was thinking of quitting right there.

I went in to see him, and he started talking about how Ken Bowman, our regular center, had got hurt before the season and how Bill Curry had to fill in and how I'd been getting high snaps on my field goal attempts. He kind of laid all the blame on Bill Curry—whom he'd already lost in the expansion draft—and made me feel like it wasn't my fault, and he just had me raring to come back in 1967. And I did, and I had my best year.

I always felt that Lombardi controlled his emotions, that he calculated them. I'm not saying he wasn't sincere —he got so absorbed in football, his son Vinny once told me, that during the season, he sometimes walked into doors—and I'm not saying he wasn't emotional, but he knew how and when to use his emotions.

Remember how you always said he'd surprise you: After you'd played a bad game, when you really expected him to rip you apart, he wouldn't be so tough. Well, I think he knew what you were expecting, and he knew how grateful you'd feel if he didn't light into you, and so he held back—he turned off his emotions—because that was more effective, in those circumstances, than getting all over you. You'd feel so good you'd be ready to tear somebody up.

Or take the way he acted the week before we played somebody like Baltimore. He felt pretty emotional about those Colt games, but he never got on us the way he did when we were getting ready to play New Orleans or Atlanta or Pittsburgh or some team in the second division. He knew we'd be up for Baltimore; he didn't have to waste his energy getting us up. But when we were facing one of those other clubs, you couldn't live with him. He had to ration his emotions; if he threw them at us every week, they'd lose their impact.

There was one thing that happened once when I was with the Giants that illustrates how he calculated his emotions. He was always on Mel Triplett, and this time, after some lecture, Triplett said to him, "Get off my back." And Lombardi said, "I won't get off your back. You get paid to play this game." And what he was saying, I think, was, "Look, my yelling at you is one of the hazards of this game, like hurting your knee or your shoulder or anything else. I don't mean anything personal, just like the guy who tackles you doesn't mean anything personal. We're both doing our jobs, and we have to get on you, and you have to take it."

Triplett came back at him, "I don't care, you get off my back," and after that, I don't think he got on Triplett so much. Again, he controlled his emotions. He still wanted to yell at Mel, he still felt the same obligation to yell, but he knew that, beyond a certain point, his yelling wasn't going to do anybody any good.

He was like that with me. After a while he realized that yelling at me didn't help anything, so he cut down on it, and from then on, we got along just fine.

Don Chandler's remarks reminded me of something Willie Davis had said a few weeks earlier. "Vince captured me," Willie said. "He earned my respect. He made me a Lombardi man. But if I didn't know him, if somebody just told me about him, I don't think I'd like him. I tend to dislike people who are too critical, who go after other people."

Donny's sentiments, I think, were similar. Personally, he didn't like being criticized. More important, he felt that he didn't respond well to criticism. We had at least one extreme example of that feeling on our club: Bill Curry, our center the year Ken Bowman got hurt. "Bill and I were alone in a car one day," Don Chandler told me, "and he was just tight as a tick. 'I'm scared to death,' he said. 'I'm scared I'm going to do something wrong.' Bill just didn't have the temperament to play for Lombardi. There's a lot of people who couldn't play for him."

"I don't really agree. I think that almost anybody could have played for Vince, and played well, and I'm including everyone from Joe Namath to Chip Oliver, the guy from the Oakland Raiders who quit pro football to go live in a commune.

I'm not suggesting that they would have converted completely to Vince's philosophy, but I think they would have converted to him; they would have come to respect and accept him, if not his ways. But it took time; Chandler didn't grow to respect Vince until his second three-year tour with him. Bill Curry spent only two seasons with the Packers, and when he left, he said he was glad to go. He said he couldn't play out of fear. Yet when Vince became ill, Curry wrote to him, a long letter, send-

ing his best wishes and apologizing for his statements, even though his statements were not so much an indictment of Vince as an indictment of Curry's own ability to adjust to Vince.

I guess it all came down to two things, two things that almost everyone who played for Vince came away with: First, he demanded at least as much of himself as he did of anyone else. Second, he was a genius in his field; more than that, his record and his style indicated that he could have been a genius in many fields. "If he'd gone to work for IBM as a bookkeeper," Don Chandler said, "I'm positive he'd be chairman of the board now."

MAX McGEE

"He's the Most Egotistical Man I've Ever Met"

Max McGee was the clown prince of the Green Bay Packers, the man who always came up with the funny line. Once, when we went through four games scoring only two touchdowns, Vince, understandably, got disgusted with our offense. He called us all together. "I must be a lousy teacher," he said. "You guys don't remember a thing." He shook his head. "We're going back to basics. Back to fundamentals." Vince reached over and picked up a ball. "Now this," he said, "is a football."

Max interrupted. "Hold on, Coach," he said. "You're going too fast."

Another time, the night before a critical game against the Cleveland Browns, Lombardi assembled the entire squad in a light rain in Cleveland Stadium. "Look at this place," he barked. "There will be more people here tomorrow than there are in the whole city of Green Bay." Vince paused. "Some of you look like you don't care," he said. "Some of you look like you're scared."

Max chimed in again. "Hell, Coach," he said, "the only thing that scares me is that the Browns may not show up."

A few years later, Vince bought a videotape setup so that he could instantly review our practices. Like several mechanical and electronic devices Vince experimented *with, this one didn't work. The first time he used it, Vince stood on the side of the field, glaring at the screen, seeing nothing but a blur, growing madder and madder. Finally, Max walked up to him. "Hey, Coach," he said, "will you lemme know when the cartoons come on?"*

Even Vince laughed.

"How'd you know when to come up with a crack?" I once asked Max.

"I could tell when Vince really didn't want to be mean," he said, "when he wanted a way out of a situation. I gave him the way out."

Max was as gifted as he was witty. During twelve seasons in Green Bay, he caught fifty touchdown passes. The only Packer to surpass him was Don Hutson, who caught 101, more than any player in the history of pro football. Max was erratic, but, almost always, the bigger the game, the better he played. He saved his finest performance— seven receptions for 138 yards and two touchdowns—for the 1967 Super Bowl game. By then, Max was thirty-four years old.

Max is now a highly successful restaurateur. He and Fuzzy Thurston operate a string of restaurants in Wisconsin, some called The Left Guard, some called The Left End. I got together with Max in the spring of 1970, at his bachelor's pad—his boar's nest—in Appleton, Wisconsin.

In 1959, Vince's first year, Howie Ferguson, our fullback, and I got to camp a couple of days before we had to. We ate dinner in the team dining room, then went out and got in a normal night of drinking. We woke up the next morning and decided to go get another free meal.

As we started into the dining room for breakfast, Lombardi grabbed us and pulled us into his office. "You start working out today," he shouted, "and you start keeping curfew today. As far as I'm concerned, when you ate a meal here yesterday, you became a part of this camp. Therefore, you abide by all my rules."

"What the hell you talking about?" said Fergy, who was kind of a wild man. "We don't have to report for two more days."

Vince exploded. "Listen, mister," he said, "you get your ass out there on the field—or you get your ass out of here!"

The two of them began screaming at each other, and I just stood there quietly, listening. I never got a word in. You know, you meet a guy for the first time—we'd never even seen him before—and he starts chewing your ass out, yelling and hollering, and you feel kind of funny. I was thinking maybe I ought to go somewhere else.

The next day or so, he had his first meeting with the full team, and he told us how tough he was going to be, and then he said, "If any of you guys don't want to be a part of the Green Bay Packers, if any of you want to be traded, just let me know. I don't want anybody here who doesn't want to be here."

Right after that speech, he called me into his office—I don't know why he picked me; maybe it was because I was one of the few established players he had—and told me he didn't know what was going to happen. He said he was scared to death that everybody was going to walk out on him. But he said he knew that if they stayed, he had them. Of course, everybody did stay, and from then on, he had us.

By the time we'd been in camp a week or so, all the guys were grumbling and saying they hated Lombardi, but I think ninety percent of them were lying. I know I never disliked the man. Right from the first meeting, I had respect for him, and it became a lot more than respect. I understood him and I admired him and I liked him. I knew how much he wanted to win, and I felt the same way. The first league game he coached in Green Bay, we beat the Chicago Bears and I had a good day, and he ran up to me afterward and planted a big kiss on my mouth.

My main problem with Vince was the same one just about everyone had: I couldn't stand being embarrassed in front of my teammates. I may not act it all the time, but, basically, I'm a shy guy. I've got to be accepted. When he chewed me out in front of my friends, I felt like a complete ass.

I never said a word back to him in that situation. I don't remember if I ever told him how I felt, but I know he didn't tell me off too often in front of everyone. If he'd been on me all the time, like he was on Hornung and Taylor and Thurston and you, I'd have quit. I'd have gone someplace else. I guess he understood that.

Still, we had our battles. Baltimore used to be kind of a pigeon for me, but one year, for some reason, he benched me just before we played the Colts. We didn't talk for an entire week. We were both stubborn. Neither of us wanted to go make up to the other. Anyway, at halftime, we were getting beat so bad, Hornung and Taylor asked Lombardi to put me in.

Just as the Colts were getting ready to kick off, he came over next to me and said, "You want to play football?"

Of course I did, but I wasn't going to tell him. "I don't care," I said.

That was the smartest thing I could have said. "Get your ass in there," he hollered. "You're gonna play this half whether you want to or not."

The maddest he ever got at me—for something that happened on the field—was during another Baltimore game. We were moving the ball well against the Baltimore zone, and I got shaken up and came out for a while, and then he sent me back in with a play. He told me to tell Bart that I was going to run a square-out and Tom Moore was going to run a deep turn-in and that he should throw the ball to Moore because the defender was going to be underneath, looking for the square-out. I gave the message to Bart, and he called the play, but instead of going deep, he threw to me. Don Shinnick, the defender, was looking for the square-out and he intercepted and ran the ball back, and that cost us the game and maybe the championship that year. I could see Lombardi think-

132

ing, "That damn McGee went in and told Bart to call his number."

When I got back to the bench, Vince was white. He gave me a look that's worse than 900 words, the look that implies that you are a no-good idiot, a stupid sonuvabitch. I guess it was better than having him scream at me, because if he'd screamed, every person in the stands would have heard him. After the game, he got me in his office and started ripping me up and down. "Wait a minute," I said. "I don't want to put the bug on someone's else's back, but I called the exact play you put in, and I told him where you wanted him to throw the ball. Hell, I can't throw the ball for him." I don't know if Vince ever believed me, but later, when Bart wrote his book, he talked about the play and said it was his fault.

During my last season, when I wasn't playing too often, Vince gave me as good an ass-chewing as I'd ever gotten. We were beating somebody real bad, and I got in the game, and Elijah Pitts broke loose on a swing pass. I was way down field, and I moved up to help block, and I saw four big sonsabitches chasing Elijah. I figured I could pick off one of them without too much trouble, or I could throw myself at them sideways and get them all. Of course, if I did that, I'd be sure to get a couple of ribs broken and maybe my knees damaged. While I was thinking about how fragile I am, Pitts shot right past me, and those four big guys came at me. I dodged all of them. I missed them on purpose. Vince called me into his office the next day and really let me have it.

He knew I wasn't wild about contact. I'd had several brain concussions, and I didn't want any more.

I'll bet you didn't know that I never did the nutcracker drill. I didn't like that drill—I didn't even like thinking about it—and when he put it in, I went to him and said, "Coach, I'm not a hitter. I can sweep-block for you, but it will not do me any good to get in that nutcracker drill and get up against Ray Nitschke and have Nitschke hit me with a forearm. You're not gaining anything by having me do that."

Vince thought it over. "I can't show any partiality," he said, "so you just get in line for that drill, and when you get near the front of the line, turn around and sneak to the end." I did that for nine years; I never once got into the nutcracker drill. We had that agreement.

Vince and I never had any real fights over my contract. I was always a little insecure, and I used to tell him, "You give me whatever you want to. I'd rather take $5,000 less than fight with you and have you bitch at me like you do at Kramer and Taylor." He usually gave me almost the amount I wanted; he was fair.

He always confided in me and asked my opinion about things. I think, at the beginning, he didn't have that vast confidence he had after winning a few championships, and he liked to test his theories on me. I know he had great respect for my knowledge of pass defenses. When I stopped playing regularly, he used to make me stand next to him during a game and listen to his ideas, and sometimes I'd suggest plays to him. He didn't take my suggestions too often, but once in a while, he did.

The one thing we never agreed on was curfew. I once snuck out after curfew eleven straight nights without getting caught. I must hold the NFL record. I used to come into breakfast tiptoeing every morning, holding my breath, waiting for him to start screaming at me and telling me that he'd double-checked my room after curfew and caught me.

He did catch me sometimes. Once, I snuck out with Fuzzy Thurston and Dan Currie and Jesse Whittenton, and we went down to Appleton and had a couple of drinks at The Left Guard, and coming back, I got stopped for speeding. I got a ticket and was told to report to court a couple of weeks later. Well, the next week we went down to New Orleans to play St. Louis in an exibition, and they kicked the hell out of us. We came back on a Sunday, and the Green Bay *Press-Gazette* had two headlines: "ST. LOUIS KNOCKS OFF THE PACK" and "MC GEE GOING TO COURT FOR LATE-NIGHT SPEEDING." I went and found every paper in the training camp and hid them so he wouldn't see the headline. But somebody sent him the paper with the story circled, and when Lombardi got hold of me, he actually seemed happy. "You thought you were gonna get away with it, didn't you?" he said. "See? There's no way you can beat me. And that's gonna cost you a thousand." The previous time he'd caught me, he'd fined me five hundred, and he'd warned me that the next time would cost me a thousand. That was when he said, "Hell, you find anything worth sneaking out for, for $1,000, call me and I'll go with you."

"Yeah," I told him. "You got me."

Then I went to Fuzzy and Dan and Jesse, and said, "Now, listen, we can work this out. You guys just give me $250 apiece toward the fine, and I won't turn you in. OK?" They did it. They helped me pay my fine. They were happy to.

Even at the end of my career, I was still fighting him over curfew. He couldn't believe that at the age of thirty-four, I still had the energy to keep sneaking out after hours. It wasn't that I wanted to defy him. Hell, no. It was just that there are certain urges that are stronger than football. One year in training camp, he was being extra strict, and Paul and I were locked up for a few weeks, no broads, no booze, till I couldn't stand it any longer. I told Paul I'd figured out how we could get some time off. At eleven o'clock that night, when we knew someone would be coming around to check on us, we pushed our beds together, took off all our clothes and jumped into bed together. We were wrapped up together when Red Cochran opened the door. "What the hell is going on here?" he said.

Paul and I looked up, and I said, very sweetly, "Will you please tell Lombardi we've gotta get a night off?"

Red wasn't sure that we were just kidding. He looked at us kind of funny for a long time.

All the years I played football, I was always in shape. I had to be. If Lombardi taught me nothing else, he taught me how to get along without much sleep. I could fake a practice. I don't remember ever going all out one hundred percent during a practice. I'd go seventy percent and save the rest for Sunday, when I needed it.

When I wasn't playing regularly, Vince would warn me on Monday if he was planning to use me that week. He knew the life I was leading and he just wanted to make sure that I'd make it to the game on Sunday.

The craziest thing, of course, was that first Super Bowl game in 1967. I had no earthly idea I'd play in that game. Neither Paul nor I expected to get off the bench. He hadn't played in about six weeks, and I knew I wouldn't play unless Boyd Dowler got hurt. Vince put in a huge penalty that week for sneaking out, something like $5,000, and we all knew he meant it, so I don't think anybody snuck out. The night before the game, Dave Hanner checked the rooms at curfew, and I asked Hawg if he was going to double-check later. "Yep," he said. But then, as he started out of my room, he changed his mind for some reason. "Nope," Hawg said. "Won't check your room later." That was enough for me. I practically ran over him getting out of the room. I'd met some blonde the night before, and I was on my way to pay my respects. I didn't feel I was letting the team down any, because I knew there wasn't a chance in hell I'd play.

I waddled in about seven-thirty in the morning, and I could barely stand up for the kickoff. On the bunch, Paul kept needling me, "What would you do if you had to play?" And I said, "No way, there's no way I could make it."

We sat together, discussing his wedding that was coming up, and, suddenly, I heard Lombardi yell, "McGee!" I figured he'd found out about my sneaking out. I figured it was about to cost me $5,000. Then he shouted, "Get in the game!" I almost fainted.

Boyd was hurt, and I played the rest of the game and caught seven passes and scored two touchdowns, and afterward, dear old Vince came up to me and said, "Nice game."

"Most any end could've done the same thing," I said.

"You're right," he said.

I looked at him, and I said, "Well, you sure took the edge off that, you sonuvabitch."

Vince and I were actually a lot alike. I think we were both interested in personal goals. I knew I wanted to be the star of every game I played. I would have played pro football for nothing but the recognition and adulation. I loved all the guys, but I wasn't a real team man, and I think Vince was the same way. He loved us all, too, but he wasn't interested in winning for *us*. He wanted the glory and the acclaim, and he wanted to be known as the man who made the Packers champions. He's got to be the most egotistical man I've ever met. I swear he preached humility to enhance his own ego. I don't blame him. Like I say, we're a lot alike.

The year Vince stopped coaching and became general manager was the same year I stopped playing. I used to sit up in the press box with him and watch the games, and I could sense at times that he did not want the Packers to win. I felt that he would have been content if the Packers had lost all fourteen games. I can understand how he felt because I felt exactly the same way. I found myself thinking at times that I didn't want them to win, either. I liked to think that I made them win, that I was the difference between victory and defeat. If I felt that way—and I was just a small part of the whole thing—can you imagine how Vince felt?

I was surprised by a couple of things Max said. First, I'd never realized that he hadn't participated in the nut-cracker drills. I always thought everybody suffered through them. And second, I'd never suspected that Max was afraid of Vince, that he hated to be embarrassed by him. I always thought nothing bothered Max—except maybe physical contact.

But I wasn't really surprised by what Max said about Vince in the press box, almost pulling for the Packers to lose. That was completely natural. I know I had the same feeling the following year, watching Gale Gillingham play-

ing right guard, the position I'd filled for a decade. I like Gilly, I think he's a great ballplayer, but I wasn't exactly upset when I saw him miss a block or mess up an assignment. If I'd felt that he was doing a better job than I'd ever done, it probably would have killed me.

FUZZY THURSTON

"He Was a Part of Me on the Field"

After dinner each night during training camp, our rookies were told to get up and sing, partly to boost their spirits, partly to amuse the veterans and mostly to entertain Vince. It was one of the few times when he was able to relax, and he seemed to enjoy an enthusiastic song as much as he did a good, crisp block. The man who organized the singing each year was Fuzzy Thurston, and he led off many sessions with his own version of "He's Got the Whole World in His Hands."

Fuzzy came up with dozens of different stanzas: "He's got the Heisman baby in his hands . . . He's got the greatest guards in his hands . . . He's got the Super Bowl champions in his hands." When Paul Hornung returned from his one-year suspension, Fuzzy sang, "He's got the gamblin' man in his hands."

Fuzzy and I filled the two guard positions during most of Vince's reign in Green Bay. He made All-Pro a couple of times, and once, in 1962, we both made All-Pro. "There are two good reasons why the Green Bay Packers are the champions of the world," Fuzzy used to say, in his banquet speeches. "Jerry Kramer is one of them, and you're looking at the other."

In the spring of 1970, Fuzzy and I carried on a running conversation—we started at his place, The Left Guard

139

in Appleton, and we finished up in Oshkosh, at a restaurant in which I have an interest—a running conversation about the man who turned us into running, pulling guards, probably the most publicized pair in pro football history.

You know, Jerry, Vince put us on the map. Before us, no one ever noticed a guard. A guard never got any publicity unless he was arrested or something. I played with the Baltimore Colts, the Chicago Bears and the Philadelphia Eagles before I wound up in Green Bay, and a guard just wasn't anybody special on those teams. Their guards did straight one-on-one blocking, some drop-back pass blocking and an occasional short trap-block, and that was it.

Vince made us feel important. He let everyone know that the power sweep was the key to his offense—and that we were the key to the power sweep. We had to be quick. We had to be smart. We had to be flexible. Some coaches put the emphasis on their backs, and some on their receivers, but Vince really concentrated on his interior linemen. If we didn't produce, his offense didn't go.

The fact that he'd been a guard himself made him more conscious of us, and he helped us on everything, from the stance right on up. If I wasn't in my best stance, if my balance was a little off, he'd see it and tell me, and I'd straighten myself out.

I can still hear some of the things he used to tell us: "Keep your head up. Block with your forehead. Put your nose right in the guy's numbers." And what was that other thing he said? "The neck bone is the strangest bone in the body. You can't possibly hurt your neck bone."

He prepared us so well, and he motivated us so well, I felt he was a part of me on the field. When I made a block, I could see him making the block, and when I walked back to the huddle, he walked back next to me. I guess part of it was that I knew he was looking at us every minute, seeing everything we did. I never turned and looked at him on the sidelines—except accidentally

—because I knew that if I did, I'd see that mad look on his face, and I'd start figuring I must have done something wrong.

The only time I could relax a little was when we were down on the one- or two-yard line, as far away from him as possible, where he couldn't see us so well. Then I'd think, "Well, I'm on my own now." And the only time I'd deliberately look at him was when we got the ball over for a touchdown. Then I'd turn and see his arm up in the air, and the grin on his face, and I'd know that, for a change, he was happy with something we'd done.

There was always a gap between Vince and me. Maybe he made it, maybe I made it, maybe it was just because I was in such awe of him, but, whatever the reason, it existed. It started the day I reported, back in 1959, after the rest of you had been in camp about four days. In the space of three days, my wife had a baby, I drove from my home in Wisconsin to Baltimore, I found out I'd been traded and I drove all the way back to Wisconsin. I went from a championship team, the Colts, to a last-place team, and when I showed up, Vince didn't pay any attention to me. I think he said hello, but he didn't even bother to shake hands. I was tired and upset and disappointed, and then to meet a man who gave absolutely no indication of what he thought of me, well, it had to irritate me.

I didn't help our relationship any by going into the restaurant business early in my career in Green Bay. Vince didn't like that. He felt a football player shouldn't have anything on his mind but football.

It wasn't that I disliked him. Hell, if I had to sum him up in a single sentence, I'd call him a dynamic, beautiful man. I respected him; I thought he had super knowledge of football, and I thought he was a fantastic organizer, putting great players and a great coaching staff together. I learned from him; he taught me to be a winner, to never be satisfied unless I was the best, and I'll never be able to repay him for that. But I just couldn't get close to him personally; I felt that he never relaxed with me, and as a result, I was never able to relax with him.

He scared me. He scared me by embarrassing me in front of my friends. He was extra tough on you and me, Jerry, because we were guards, because we played his position. He chewed us more than he chewed anyone else. I suppose he felt that we needed it, and he felt, too, that we could take it, but, I'll tell you, I almost couldn't. Each time he screamed at me in a meeting, I sort of closed my ears. I tried to let it pass through me. I tried to forget everything he said. But I always felt miserable, and I hated him for doing it in front of everyone. If he'd told me the same things privately, I wouldn't have cared so much. But every time he cut me up in front of my friends, I swore that I'd never play for him again. I swore that I'd get myself traded or I'd go home and never come back again. I felt that way about fourteen times a year, for nine years.

There's no doubt about the angriest I ever saw him. That's one thing that'll stand out in my mind for the rest of my life. It was when he showed us the movies of the Detroit game on Thanksgiving Day, 1962. The Lions beat us, 26–14, the only game we lost that year, including exhibitions, playoffs, everything.

He started yelling the moment the movie started, and even when the movie stopped, he didn't. He yelled at us while we got dressed for practice, and he yelled at us while we practiced. He made us do more up-downs than we'd ever done before. He was angry for four straight hours, and not once, during those four hours, did the bitterness and hate come off his face.

He said it was the most disgusting example of football he'd ever seen in his life. He said that you and I pulled like dogs, we pass-blocked like dogs and that we never did one thing any guard should do in the NFL. That was the year we both made All-Pro, and he said, "All-Pro? You two look like All-Horse Manure to me."

I hated him that day. I hated him right up till the next Sunday, when we killed the Los Angeles Rams.

142

After the 1967 season, I was thinking about playing in 1968, and I bumped into him at the annual 1,000-Yard Club banquet. He looked at me and he said, "By the way, Fuzzy, when are you going to announce your retirement?"

He was telling me to retire, and he really hurt me. I hated him then, too, hated him for telling me I was through. He could have called me into his office and talked it over with me, something private, instead of telling me at a dinner I should quit.

But, you know, I thought a lot about it afterward, and he was right. It was time for me to retire. I just didn't like the way he did it.

In 1968, I watched some games with him from the press box, and I saw him at a few cocktail parties, and the barrier between us came down a little. Finally, I reached the point where I could kid about him making me quit after the 1967 season: I figured he knew that if I'd stayed on, after he'd stepped down, we would have kept right on winning.

Despite the harsh feelings he sometimes had toward Vince, Fuzzy, who was born and raised in Wisconsin, was one of the people most saddened when Vince left the Packers. "I'm a Green Bay person and I always want to see the Packers win," Fuzzy said. "I hated to lose him. It was like losing an era."

JIMMY TAYLOR

"All He Wanted From You Was Perfection"

One Tuesday morning in Green Bay, after we had beaten some team by fewer points than Vince thought we should have, he walked into the movie session with a scowl on his face, looking for something to holler about. One of the guys' wives had just had a baby, and he'd handed out cigars to everyone. Jimmy Taylor was sitting four or five rows from the front of the room, waiting for the films and the fury, puffing on a big cigar.

Vince pounced on him. "Taylor!" he yelled. "You don't have the face for a cigar! Get rid of it!"

Jimmy got rid of it.

At one time or another, Vince jumped on Jimmy Taylor for just about everything you could imagine. But Jimmy seemed to thrive on Vince's abuse. He paid him back with great football.

For five straight years, from 1960 through 1964, Jimmy gained more than 1,000 yards rushing. In 1962, his finest season, he led the National Football League in rushing and in scoring, was named the league's Most Valuable Player and was the unanimous All-Pro fullback, ahead of his arch rival, Cleveland's Jimmy Brown.

In 1965, troubled by injuries, Jimmy had an off-season. But in the NFL championship game, against Cleveland, he outgained Brown, ninety-six yards to fifty, and we out-

144

scored the Browns, 23–12. Jimmy won the Most Valuable Player award.

That performance helped trigger the most serious dispute between Jimmy and Vince. In 1966, the two of them couldn't agree on contract terms, and Jimmy decided to play out his option. In 1967, he shifted to the New Orleans Saints. Vince deeply resented Jimmy's departure, and he did not hide his resentment.

The same year, Vince lost Paul Hornung to the Saints in the expansion draft—because of a lingering neck injury, Paul never got to play in New Orleans—and when we reported to training camp in Green Bay, Vince finished his welcoming speech with praise for Paul and a barb for Jimmy:

"We're going to miss Paul Hornung. We're going to miss Paul a great deal. He was a leader and he added a lot of spice to professional football. We're all going to miss him.

"We will replace the other fellow."

When Jimmy and I sat down at his home in Baton Rouge a few days after the 1970 Super Bowl, I asked him if he thought Vince had any weaknesses. Dixie Taylor, Jimmy's wife, was listening in. "His only weakness," she said, "was football."

You remember the time Vince forgot his anniversary? I guess Marie must've chewed him out good, and for the next two or three days, he took it all out on us. He was miserable. We all went and wrote down his anniversary so that we could remind him in case he ever forgot again.

As long as I knew he could scream at me for something like that—for something *he'd* done wrong—he couldn't bother me too much. He yelled a lot, but his words usually didn't cut me. One day, he gave me one of those lectures, you know, "I made you, mister, and you'd be nothing without me," and I said to him, "Yeah, Coach, but you can't run with the ball."

He began to sputter. "No, I can't run with the ball,"

he said. "But I coach this team, and if I don't get the ball for you, you can't carry it."

And I just said, "Well, if you want to carry it sometime, go ahead," and he didn't have much to say to that.

I think we really got along well. We agreed on almost everything. He believed in minimizing mistakes, and I couldn't argue with that. When he yelled at you for something you did, it was because you'd done it wrong. All he wanted from you was perfection.

He made us practice the same thing over and over until we got it down perfect, and I never minded that. When I was a kid, I used to practice football and basketball seven, eight, nine hours a day, so how could I complain?

He believed in ball control, and so did I; that gave me more chances to run with the ball. He put a lot of emphasis on conditioning, and that was fine with me. I ran during the off-season, and I did isometrics, so I didn't have to worry at all about getting out of shape.

He tried to push you beyond what you thought were your limits, and I went along with that. Whenever I thought I was out of strength, I always found some somewhere. I used to push myself so hard doing my isometrics that I wouldn't stop until I'd popped blood vessels in my head from straining so much.

He taught you to be angry, and to use all your anger against your opponents, and I did. I hated them—from the opening kickoff to the final whistle. I loved to take the battle to them, to sting them, to go right at them and pick up the extra yard. I figured I couldn't out-cute them, so I just ran over them. Besides, I always got a bigger kick out of running over them than I got out of running around them.

He didn't believe in injuries. He instilled in you the feeling that you can push yourself so you don't notice a bruise or a charley horse or something like that. And even if it hurt, even if you were suffering some pain, he instilled in you the feeling that you couldn't get reinjured. He'd say, "You can't hurt a charley horse. The more you push it and drive it and work on it, the more you put circulation back in the individual cells that have been injured." I believed him.

Vince and I were pretty much in tune, except at contract time. Every year, I'd sit down with him and tell him how much I deserved, and he'd tell me how much he thought I was worth, and, usually, there'd be a good difference. Sometimes we'd just sit there in his office, and neither of us would say a word for a long time. He'd be waiting for me to give in, and I'd be waiting for him, and then we'd end up working out some kind of compromise. We had a fight just about every year, but we always got it settled.

Then, after the 1965 season, after I'd had that good day against the Browns in the championship game, I decided I probably didn't have too many years left, and I wanted one last big contract. I wanted a three-year contract up in the $70,000, $80,000 class.

He was willing to give me the money I wanted, but he'd only let me have a one-year contract. I wouldn't give in. "I've done a lot for you," he'd say, and I'd say, "I've done a lot for you, too." I told him I was going to play out my option, play one season at my old salary and then be a free agent, free to negotiate with any other team.

I played that 1966 season at about half the salary he would've given me on a one-year contract. He was on me all year, trying to get me to sign, needling me and sweet-talking me and talking to Dixie, everything he could think of. He made some offers it must've hurt him to make, but he wouldn't come up with that three-year contract.

I had a pretty good season, and by the time we won the NFL championship and the first Super Bowl game, Vince was willing to give me a three-year contract.

But by then, the stakes had gone up. New Orleans was in the picture, getting ready to field its first team in 1967, and the Saints wanted me badly. I came from Baton Rouge and I'd played my college ball at LSU, and they figured I'd be a big gate attraction down here. They made me a fantastic offer, so good I just couldn't turn it down. Vince made one last offer, but it wasn't even close. I went and signed with New Orleans, and Vince was pretty bitter.

I never spoke to him that whole year, while I was playing in New Orleans and he was coaching you guys. I was having a rough year with the Saints—I don't think I saw a hole at the line of scrimmage once all year —and you were fighting for the championship, and I suppose he felt that I'd run out on him, that I'd deserted him. I missed Green Bay, and I sure missed the blocking, but there was no way I could've turned down that New Orleans offer.

In the spring of 1968, after he'd given up the coaching job, I went to Wisconsin for the 1,000-Yard Club banquet, and before the dinner, I went up to see him. You brought me up. I guess you wanted us to make up. He wasn't too happy to see me. "You could have called me," he said. "That's the least you could have done before you signed with them."

"Coach," I said, "you're hard to get ahold of."

He seemed to soften up a little toward me then.

A couple of months later, they had that Vince Lombardi Day up in Green Bay, and I was in training camp and couldn't get there, but Dixie and I sent a telegram, saying best wishes to a man who really deserves it, something like that.

I had a bad exhibition season—I just couldn't cut it anymore—and before the opening game of the 1968 season, I retired. That was the end of my active football career. But I still had that contract, and the Saints gave me a front-office job.

When the Saints went up to Milwaukee to play the Packers, I went up, too, and I sat in the press box with Vince. He told me then that he was going to be leaving Green Bay, that he was going to get back into coaching. We would have loved to have had him come down here.

Then he made the decision to go to Washington, and his first league game, coaching the Redskins, was against
148

the Saints here, and I saw him then, and it was all forgotten. We were friends again. I guess with his big Washington contract, he could understand what I'd done a little better. And the fact that he beat the Saints didn't hurt any, either.

Dixie got a chance to talk with Marie for a while, and Marie told her that Paul and Max had been up to Washington and that when they were talking with Vince, he'd mentioned something about what a good fullback I'd been. "Why didn't you ever tell Jimmy that?" Max asked him.

"Well," he said. "Jimmy knows I feel that way."

I guess I do. But I still wish he'd told me.

Jimmy was one of a handful of Green Bay players who had serious disagreements with Vince, and the result was always the same: He stayed, and they left. The amazing thing isn't that Vince had players rebel—every coach faces that—but that every single player, after he left Vince, still respected him, still praised him.

The classic case was Jim Ringo, an All-Pro center for eight straight years. When Ringo gave Vince a salary ultimatum in 1964, Vince traded him, shipped him from our championship team to the last-place Philadelphia Eagles. Ringo could, understandably, be bitter; after all, he was All-Pro before he played for Vince, and he was All-Pro after he played for Vince. Now he is a line coach for the Chicago Bears. "I teach pure Lombardi," Ringo says, "Every day I coach, I appreciate him more and more."

BILL AUSTIN

"Success Hasn't Spoiled Him; It's Made Him Greater"

If Vince Lombardi's coaching heritage could be neatly plotted like the blood lines of a thoroughbred, the chart would be a formplayer's dream. By Earl Blaik, out of Jim Crowley, with a straight line back to Knute Rockne, spiced by a splash of Frank Leahy, a trace of Sid Gillman, a dash of Tom Landry and a distant relationship to the Paul-Brown-Ara-Parseghian-Weeb-Ewbank-Miami-of-Ohio coaching clan, Vince had the breeding of a Kentucky Derby favorite.

But like a Triple Crown champion who flopped at stud, Vince did not turn out assistants who followed him to the winner's circle—at least not so far. Four of his Green Bay assistants have gone on to become head coaches—Norb Hecker, Phil Bengtson, Tom Fears and Bill Austin—and among them, in ten collective NFL seasons, they have posted only one barely winning record, Phil Bengtson's 8–6 mark in Green Bay in 1969. To be fair, each of them has labored under a handicap. Hecker and Fears launched expansion teams, Austin inherited a weak Pittsburgh squad and Bengtson got the Packers as the club was coming down from its peak.

Of all his assistants who graduated to higher jobs, Bill Austin strikes me as the one most similar to Vince. Perhaps it is because Bill, like Vince, was a guard in his playing days; perhaps it is because Bill's apprenticeship under Vince was the lengthiest, spanning eleven seasons, five as an active player in New York and then six as an assistant coach in Green Bay.

Bill left Green Bay after the 1964 season, spent a year as an assistant with the Los Angeles Rams, then took command of the Steelers in 1966. Bill suffered through three losing seasons in Pittsburgh, but he had one consolation: In none of his three years was the team's record quite so poor as it was either the year before he arrived (2–12) or the year after he left (1–13).

And Bill, who returned to Vince as the offensive line coach of the Redskins in 1969, had one golden souvenir of his Steeler days: In the final game of the 1967 season, Bill became the first—and only—former assistant to beat the master. The Steelers whipped us, 24–17. "I took a great deal of pride in that," Bill says.

Vince was in the hospital when the 1970 training camps opened, and Bill Austin became Washington's acting head coach. I visited with him at the Redskin camp in Carlisle, Pennsylvania, only a couple of weeks before Vince died, only a couple of weeks before Bill became, officially, the team's head coach.

When Vince got to the Giants, he was accustomed to having the players in the palm of his hand, the way they'd been up at West Point. He was full of vim, vigor and vitality, and right away, he got after Eddie Price, our fullback. Eddie was a great running back, and Vince chewed him out for his blocking or something like that, and Eddie listened a while, then said, "Enough of this, boy. I'm quitting the game." He just took off across the field for the dressing room. And Vince went running after him, like a little puppy dog, yelling, "Eddie, Eddie, come back, come back!"

And Eddie said, "Go to hell!"

It was really a comical scene, and we've kidded Vince about it ever since. He never imagined that a player

151

might just run away from him; no cadet would have done it.

Vince was a great offensive coach for the Giants. He put some imagination into our offense, including an early version of the Green Bay power sweep. He was just as intense in those days as he was later in Green Bay. One day, Marie drove him to practice, and a friend went along for the ride. The friend sat in the front seat, between Vince and Marie. Vince didn't say a word during the ride; he was so intent thinking about football. When he reached the stadium, he opened the car door, turned, said, "Thanks, honey," and kissed the guy sitting next to him.

Another time, after a practice session, Vince showered and put on his socks and his shirt and his shoes and his jacket and his overcoat and started to walk out of the stadium. The man at the gate stopped him. "Excuse me, Mr. Lombardi," he said, "but I think you should go back and put your pants on."

He's so involved in football, emotionally and physically, that he becomes oblivious to everything else. God, he hates to get beat. He doesn't want to be second in anything. We used to kid him, "Hell, you'd cheat at gin to beat your own mother."

A lot of people misinterpret his intensity, his desire. Just about everyone has the idea that he's one of the toughest and most cold-hearted men in the world, but it's just not true. He's got the biggest heart I've ever seen. He hated to cut people from his teams; it killed him every time he had to do it, so he finally got someone to do it for him. If you're a friend of his, you're a friend for life. And if he doesn't like you, forget it. But I don't know of too many people that he really doesn't like. Of course, he's got that Italian temper. He was once arguing football with Johnny Sauer, who coached with him at West Point, and he went and slapped Johnny in the face; Johnny told me that story, and he loves Vince, and he understands him. He'll scream and holler at someone, and then a few minutes later you'll ask him who he was yelling at, and he won't remember.

He hasn't really changed over the years. Success hasn't spoiled him; it's made him greater. He beams with success. He fills up with enthusiasm, and that's when you hear that laugh, that infectious laugh of his. I know he's not perfect. He's a very domineering person, which is part of the reason I left Green Bay and went to Los Angeles; I felt I needed a change then. But over the years, I've developed a great love and admiration for him. I admire his principles. I admire his methods. You're always treated fairly by him. I just love to work for the man.

It's funny. I've known him sixteen years now, and I've never really socialized with him. He doesn't believe in socializing with people who work for him, and I can see why. We spend so much time together, he must get sick of us.

Vince loves to have a good time, but he has to do all his entertaining at home. When he goes out, somebody's always running up to him and tugging on his arm and telling him how he can improve his offense. He can't go anyplace without being recognized and bothered.

I remember I did go out with him once. One year, when he was the head coach in the Pro Bowl in Los Angeles, he took me and Phil Bengtson along as assistants. Marie wasn't on the trip, and one night my wife and I and the Bengtsons and Vince went out on the Sunset Strip and saw a few shows and had a good, relaxed time. Then my wife and I drove Vince back to the Biltmore Hotel downtown. I had to go around back to the parking lot, so, to save Vince a walk, I let him off by the side of the hotel. My wife and I said goodnight to him there.

The next morning, at breakfast, Vince walked up to me, looking like he had a bit of a headache, and said, "Don't you ever leave me off on the side of a hotel again. I didn't know which way to go. I turned and went the wrong way and walked five blocks looking for the hotel. I had to call a cab to get me back."

That was the last time we went out together.

Here in Washington last year, I think we worked even longer hours than we used to work in Green Bay. It took him a while to realize that we just didn't have the people we had in Green Bay, and once he realized it, he tried to make up for it with hard work. It was frustrating. Sometimes, after a bad practice, he'd look at me and say, "Why the hell did I ever come back to this?" But then he'd bring himself back up again and start fighting the problem all over, and he'd be as enthusiastic as he was those early years in Green Bay.

We did have a few lighter moments during the season. At one point, we realized that one of our halfbacks, Larry Brown, was slow getting off the ball when he was on one side of the formation. On the other side, he was fine. We discovered the problem was that Larry was deaf in one ear, and when he was out on the side where his deaf ear was closer to the quarterback, he wasn't hearing the signals. We got a hearing aid and put it in the deaf side of his helmet with a wire transmitting to the good ear. And then we decided to test it.

Vince and I were in the dressing room, and we called Larry in and told him to put on the helmet. Then Vince said to him, "Now, Larry, you go in the corner and I'll whisper and we'll see if you can hear me."

Larry moved into the corner, and Vince whispered something and then said, "Did you hear me?"

"Coach," Larry said, "I never had any trouble hearing you. It's the quarterback I can't hear."

Vince did a magnificent job with Sonny Jurgensen. Sonny has a great arm—Vince has publicly called him the greatest quarterback he's ever seen—and Vince sold him completely on the Green Bay style passing attack. He sold him on short passes, on safe passes. He sold him on everything, except one thing. Vince tried all year to persuade Sonny to back up into the pocket, to keep facing the secondary instead of turning sideways and going back. Sonny didn't like backing out. Anyway, we were playing Philadelphia in the second half of the season, and we had a pass situation coming up, and Sonny remembered

Vince wanted him to back out of the line. He went back about eight to ten yards and fell flat over backwards and, of course, the defenders clobbered him. Sonny called a time-out and came over to the sidelines to check on the next play, and he looked at Vince and said, "Now, what the hell do you think of your backing out?"

Vince started laughing so hard he couldn't give Sonny a play. That's one of the few times I've ever seen Vince Lombardi laugh during a football game.

I can't say enough about the man. He's honest. He's firm. He's smart. He's sincerely interested in people. You know what I say when people ask me what Vince Lombardi is really like? I always tell them that if Vince were a ditchdigger, in about two or three weeks, he'd be the foreman, and six weeks later, he'd own the company. He'd be on top. It's the only place he belongs.

Before I left Bill Austin, I asked him if he thought Vince would have been able to win a divisional championship in Washington. Bill didn't hesitate. "Yes," he said.

"When?" I asked.

"This year."

I had to feel sorry for Bill. He has some act to follow.

BOB LONG

"We Even Miss His Screaming"

When Bob Long arrived in Green Bay in 1964, he had only one year of college football behind him. He had been primarily a basketball player at Wichita University, but, in his senior year, he had decided to try football. Swift and sure-handed, he was so impressive as a pass catcher that Vince drafted him in the fourth round for 1964.

Bob never got to play much in Green Bay. Troubled by a knee injury and playing behind such proven wide receivers as Boyd Dowler, Max McGee and Carroll Dale, Bob caught only twenty-five passes in four years.

Shortly before the start of the 1968 season, Green Bay traded him to Atlanta. Midway through the year, he was leading the Falcons in pass receptions, and then, on Interstate Highway 75 in Georgia, he was in an automobile crash. Another car jumped the divider and slammed into Bob's car, driving the engine into him. Bob broke his right foot, knee cap and hip, three vertebrae on the right side of his back and his right elbow. As he lay in the hospital, there was considerable doubt that he would ever be able to run again. Football, Bob decided, was out of the question.

But in the summer of 1969, Vince persuaded him to come out of retirement and acquired him for the Washing-

ton Redskins. Bob responded by catching forty-eight passes—more than he had caught in all of his five previous professional seasons—and by placing fourteenth among National Football League receivers. He had more receptions, incidentally, than any Green Bay end.

When the Redskins went to Cincinnati for an exhibition game before the 1970 season, I went with them. The day before the game, Bob Long and I met in my hotel room and talked about the man who had refused to give up on him.

I wasn't one of Vince's favorites in Green Bay. When I hurt my knee during a scrimmage before the 1966 season, he yelled, "Drag him off the field and let's get on with the scrimmage."

I had a torn cartilage in the knee, but for six weeks he made me keep playing. He told me that there was nothing wrong with my leg. He made me think I could play, and I did, but I hated him for it. Everyone who's ever played for him has hated him at one time or another. I was giving him my blood and sweat, and it didn't seem like it was enough.

Then the doctors operated on me. The surgeon told me it was one of the worst torn cartilages he'd ever seen.

Outside of yelling at me about my knee, I don't think Vince talked to me ten or fifteen minutes during my four years in Green Bay. Then, last summer, he called me up and asked me to come back and play for him. He must've talked to me for half an hour on the phone. I really thought I was finished. I told him I couldn't run, and I was depressed, mentally and physically.

He said he knew all about my problems. He said he knew how I felt about Norm Van Brocklin, my coach in Atlanta. "Don't worry about that," he said. "My feelings about him are the same as yours." He said that even though I'd been hurt, I'd still be able to help him, and he said he'd help me, mentally and physically. I told him I'd spent four years sitting on the bench for him, and he said he wasn't asking me to come back to sit on the bench. He said I'd be a starter. In his own way, I guess, he was apologizing to me for making me play when I had that torn cartilage.

When Vince Lombardi asks you to come back and play for him, that has got to be the greatest compliment you can receive as a football player and as a man. I told him I'd come back. What else could I do? We settled the contract right then, on the phone.

He treated me beautifully in Washington. When I arrived, he was smiling and he was sincerely glad to see me. I was a part of his past. I was a reminder of his championship years. He knew that I was hurting, and he told me to go at my own pace. It was some change from Green Bay. Suddenly, I was one of his favorites. I was only half the receiver, physically, that I'd been in Green Bay, but I worked like hell for him. I gave him everything I had.

It was a whole different world from Green Bay. We had some really fine superstars like Sonny Jurgensen and Jerry Smith and Charley Taylor—and we had some good offensive linemen, but we didn't have any depth. Our special teams—the kick and return teams—were horrible. Remember how Vince always said that the special teams were a test of courage? Well, in Washington, every time we kicked off, we knew we were in danger of a long return.

Out in Green Bay, we'd been so deep in people that Vince had to cut good players. One of the last guys he cut in 1967 was Mike Bass. Mike put out 110 per cent in Green Bay, but he was a defensive halfback, competing against guys like Herb Adderley and Bob Jeter and John Rowser, and Vince had to cut him. Mike came on the field crying the day he was cut. He thanked Vince for giving him a chance, and then he went to Detroit and was on their taxi squad a couple of years. When the Lions released him last year, Vince remembered him, remembered how hard he'd tried and picked him up. He was a fine cornerback for us last year. But Vince had to scramble to come up with players like that.

At Green Bay, his players very seldom made mistakes, mental or physical. In Washington, I would constantly see guys making mental mistakes. Lombardi would yell and scream until he got blue in the face, and they would continue to make the same mistakes. He would shake his head and stop yelling. He hollered more in Green Bay than he did here.

Vince laughed more here, and he was closer to the players than he'd ever been in Green Bay. Maybe it was because we didn't have the talent, and he knew that we were giving him our best. It probably would've been different in a year or two if we'd been competing for the title. Last year, he'd come into the locker room and joke and laugh and tell stories. You could tell how happy he was to be back coaching. He'd light up every time somebody called him "Coach."

He talked about Green Bay a lot, and he showed us Packer films over and over and over. I heard several of the guys say they were getting sick and tired of hearing about Green Bay, but I think that they were very small individuals. They were seeing the best.

His main objective was to instill in all the guys the feeling that they could win, and to do it, he had to approach every game like it was the Super Bowl. He made us believers. We were in every game we played except the Baltimore game. That was the only one that we lost by more than thirteen points. I honestly believe if we'd won the Cleveland game, our second game of the year—they beat us, 27–23—we would have gone on to win the Eastern championship. Out of our first six games, that was the only one we lost. If we'd won it, our confidence would have grown so much nobody would have stopped us.

We miss him now. It's such a big void. Sonny's a great leader on the field, and Bill Austin's a great coach, but it's not the same. How could it be? You don't find a man like him very often. We miss Vince at dinner time, at practice, in the locker room, on the plane, on the bus. We even miss his screaming at the equipment man and at the bus driver.

You know, when the season began last year, some of the players who'd been here a while started out hating him. But as the season progressed, they stopped bitching and started praising him. By the end of the year, they all loved him—every single one of them.

During my visit to the Redskin camp, I sat down one day with Carl Kammerer. Carl had been the team's defensive captain, the starting end, before Vince arrived. Under Vince, he spent a good part of the 1969 season on the bench. If anyone had a logical reason to be displeased with Vince, it was Kammerer. I mentioned Vince's illness —he was hospitalized then—and Carl slammed a fist into the palm of his hand. "There are so many no-good sonsabitches in this world," he said. "Why does something like this have to happen to such a great man?"

Ironically, a few weeks after Vince died, a few weeks after the entire Washington team flew up to New York City for the funeral, the Redskins released Bob Long. A few weeks later, he signed on with the Los Angeles Rams, his pro career still miraculously alive.

160

SAM HUFF

"The Only Reason I Came Back to Football Was to Be With Him"

Roughly a decade ago, a television show called "The Violent World of Sam Huff" made the middle linebacker position one of the more glamorous in pro football. Actually, it is one of the more miserable, demanding an unreasonable combination of strength, speed, stamina and courage. Few men have played the position so well as Sam Huff.

From 1956 through 1963, Huff played middle linebacker for the New York Giants. Four times in those eight years, he was All-Pro, and six times the Giants won their divisional title. The Giants shipped Huff to Washington in 1964 and, perhaps more than coincidentally, immediately slipped from first place to last. They have not had an All-Pro middle linebacker—or a winning season—since Huff departed.

Huff played four years for the Redskins, then announced his retirement from football and sat out the entire 1968 season. In 1969, Vince Lombardi—the same man who had refused to let Huff quit the Giants in his rookie year—brought Sam back for another season with the Redskins, this one as a player-coach.

In 1970, Sam Huff once again gave up playing football and became a fulltime coach with the Redskins. I chatted *with him in Cincinnati, the same day I saw Bob Long. It was the first time I'd ever really sat down with him. All the previous times I saw Sam Huff, I was trying, not always successfully, to cut his legs out from under him.*

Vince's death was imminent, and Sam was angry, "I was looking forward to this year so much," he said.

I feel sorry for the people who don't know Vince Lombardi. They've been cheated.

There is no finer human being in the world. He is one of the two greatest people I've met in my lifetime; the other was John F. Kennedy. If you could select your own father, you would want him to be like Vince.

He once said that if he picked an all-time All-Pro team, I would be the middle linebacker. I'm prouder of that than I am of anything else anyone's ever said about me. Receiving a compliment from Coach Lombardi is like receiving the crown from the king. It is absolutely the last word.

The only reason I came back to pro football last year was to be with him. No one else could have gotten me to come out of retirement. I had a terrific job, a comfortable life, a great future. I was making a lot more money than I'm making now. And then he asked me to return to Washington.

Originally, he asked me to come back strictly as a coach, and I jumped at the idea, the opportunity to work under the master. Then he called me and told me that, due to sudden complications, he had to withdraw the coaching offer. He was sorry; he was upset. Lombardi doesn't like to tell anyone bad news.

I felt badly, too, and after thinking about it for a while, I told my wife that if I couldn't go back as a coach under Vince, I'd like to go back as a player under him. She told me I was crazy, but she understood. I called Lombardi and said, "Coach, what do you think of me being a player-coach for you?"

He got all excited. "You think you can do it?" he asked.

"Hell, yes," I said.

"Then you've got a deal," Vince said. "I just hope you don't cost me too much money."

As a player-coach, I got to see Vince from two sides at the same time. I discovered that the opinion I'd had of him before I came back—a very high opinion—was wrong. My opinion was too low. He is the most dedicated, hard-working, motivating man I've ever seen. I loved every minute I spent with him last year; I even loved the grass drills.

I love football, I love the game more than anything in the world, but my dedication equals one-third of his. It's his life. I remember one time we were watching some films, Kansas City versus Green Bay in the Super Bowl. On one play, Jimmy Taylor took off through tackle and broke to the outside and went for the touchdown. I think he carried about three guys with him. Lombardi, watching, was up and screaming, "Look at that sonuvabitch run!" I guarantee he'd seen that film two hundred times, but he couldn't contain his enthusiasm.

He gave 150 per cent of himself, and he got 150 per cent out of all his players. Willie Banks, one of our guards, got hurt in a game, and his ankle swelled up three times normal size. When Willie came out on the field Tuesday morning, he was limping badly. Coach Lombardi looked at him and said, "Mister, I want to tell you something. You're not quitting on me. You're going to play next Sunday if we have to carry you out there on a stretcher. Now start running!" Willie could hardly walk, but he ran, anyway. And he played the following Sunday, and he did OK, too. It was amazing.

I was just enthralled by the man, by all his characteristics. He is in complete command of every situation. He is the only man I've ever known that, when you're talking to him, without him saying a word, you know when the conversation is over. You just know. There's no small talk. There's no wasting of time.

He's the only man I've seen who can handle Sonny Jurgensen. Sonny, without wanting to, always tests every individual he meets. He'll always try to be the dominating figure. He listened to Vince. Sonny is one of the most intelligent football players in the world, and he's been in this league for almost fifteen years, and still Coach Lombardi taught him more about playing quarterback than he ever dreamed he'd know. Vince never forced Sonny to do anything. He just got a feel of him and adjusted to him. I think Vince loves working with quarterbacks.

People think Vince is the roughest and toughest man God ever created, and he probably is. He'd stand up to anyone. But he is also one of the softest men God ever created. He loves his players as much as a man can love another man.

I remember, in 1959, the year he went out to Green Bay, we played an exhibition game in Bangor, Maine, the Giants against the Packers. Before the game, he came over to our hotel to visit with Charlie Conerly, Frank Gifford, Alex Webster and Kyle Rote, his boys, the offensive backfield. He got so choked up, he had tears in his eyes. I'll never forget it. He loved those guys.

He never held a grudge against anyone. He never wanted to hurt anyone personally. When he was screaming on the field, I don't think he ever knew who he was giving hell to. I've known the man fifteen years, and at the end of last season, we were sitting one day, all the coaches watching the films, and Vince jumped up and pointed at the screen and hollered, "That number 70's too slow! He's not moving fast enough! We got to get a new man in there!"

That's when I knew it was time for me to retire again. I was number 70.

During our conversation, Sam mentioned to me that Vince had once told him that one of his deepest desires was to leave his family one million dollars. "Coach," Sam said to Vince, "you've already given your family something that's worth a lot more than any money you could ever leave. You've given them the Lombardi name."

SONNY JURGENSEN

"I Still Feel He's With Us All the Time"

I've heard a story, perhaps apocryphal, that when John Unitas opened a restaurant called The Golden Arm, Sonny Jurgensen went up to John and said, "Thanks for naming your place after me."

Whether the story's true or not, Sonny's got a right to be proud of his arm. Before the 1970 season ends, he'll have the second greatest number of completed passes in the history of pro football, the second greatest number of yards gained and the second greatest number of touchdown passes. Of course, the fellow who owns the restaurant will still be first in all three categories.

The 1970 season is Sonny's fourteenth in the National Football League, but only once in all his years, split between Philadelphia and Washington, has he been a member of a championship team. And then, with the 1960 Eagles, he was the backup quarterback.

As a regular, after one winning season, Sonny suffered through seven straight losing seasons. But last year, under Vince Lombardi, Sonny became a winner again—and, for the second time in his pro career, the leading passer in the NFL. The most impressive statistic was his completion percentage. Before 1969, Sonny had never completed more than fifty-eight per cent of his passes in a season;

*his lifetime average was fifty-five per cent. In 1969, he
completed sixty-two per cent of his passes.*

"Vince," somebody told me, "took the greatest thrower
in football and made him the greatest passer."

*I met with Sonny Jurgensen in Washington a few days
after the Redskins opened their 1970 season. They lost
the opener in San Francisco. "We were flat," Sonny said.
"We were so flat."*

The game was played two weeks after Vince died.

I envy you, Jerry, I really do. I envy all you guys from
Green Bay. You had him for nine years. We only had
him for one—just long enough for him to educate us as
to what it takes to win.

He used to tell us the world needs heroes, but I don't
think he ever realized what a big hero he was himself. I
still feel he's with us all the time. I just wish it were
really true.

I didn't know too much about Coach Lombardi—except that you fellows were always winning—until I had a
chance to sit down with Bart Starr at a dinner a couple of
years ago. Bart told me about the intense preparation you
went through each and every week, about what a plea-
sure it was to go out and execute in a ball game
knowing that you were as well prepared as any football
team could possibly be. It was so different from what I'd
always gone through.

Then, last year, I found out for myself what Bart
meant. Coach Lombardi called me into his office once
he got settled in, and his first words to me were, "I've
heard a lot of things about you as a person and as a
player, and I'm sure you've heard a lot of things about
me. Well, that's got nothing to do with our relationship.
I just ask one thing of you: I want you to be yourself.
Don't emulate anyone else. Don't try to be someone you're
not. Just be yourself."

That was a beautiful way to start off, and as we got
going, he told me I had to be a leader, I had to set an

example, and he called upon me to do things I'd never done before. I worked harder than I'd ever worked—those grass drills just about killed me—but I had more fun than I'd ever had. At the end of the exercises each day, he'd say, "OK, Sonny, take 'em around the backstop," and I could barely stand up, but I'd lead the team running around the field. When we had our rookie show, the rookies did an imitation of that, and when the guy playing Coach Lombardi said, "OK, Sonny, take 'em around the backstop," all the guys trotted off the stage, and then they all came back, except the guy playing me. He came crawling in a little later.

He taught me things about reading defenses, about keying, that I never knew existed. I had to break a lot of bad habits. I used to force the ball, throw no matter what the coverage was. "We don't force the ball," he said, and he showed me what he meant. I used to call a play and then pick out the receiver and hit him if I could. But last year, I'd call a play, and then I'd read the defense, and depending on the defense I saw, I'd know where my receivers were going to be and where to throw the ball. I used to think it was just up to the defense to react to me. I didn't know I could react to it.

When the season was over, Coach Lombardi said to me, "You really had a great year. You completed sixty-two per cent of your passes. I really enjoyed working with you. But, you know what? I think we can complete seventy per cent of our passes next year."

And I said, "Coach, I do, too. I think we can, too." I really believed it.

He had great knowledge of football, and he did a great job of preparation, but that wasn't what made him head and shoulders above any other coach I'd ever known. Lots of coaches have knowledge, and lots of them can prepare you, give you a game plan. But he could inspire you. He could motivate you. He told us we were going to be a team. We were going to rise together or fall on our faces together. You know, we had a history of playing as individuals, and he taught us to have respect for each other.

167

We did everything last year on Lombardi Time. Once, in pre-training camp, a receiver showed up for a meeting five minutes early, which meant he was ten minutes later than everyone else. Coach Lombardi jumped on him. "Young man," he said, "you'll never play for me if you can't be on time." And that fellow didn't make the team, either.

He had a good sense of humor. Right at the beginning, he told me that I was throwing too quick, that I wasn't taking enough time before releasing the ball. I told him I wasn't exactly used to having a lot of time to throw. "Don't worry," he said. "Just take your time. We're going to give you the best pass blocking you ever saw." I kind of shook my head. I was a little skeptical.

Well, anyway, I got good protection most of the time, but one game late in the year, I got hit, the way all quarterbacks do, with just about the whole defensive line coming in on me. I was really decked, and when I came off the field, I said to him, "Hey, I thought you told me at the beginning of the year you were gonna give me the best pass blocking I ever saw."

He looked at me and said, "Well, I guess you knew the personnel better than I did."

And he gave me that laugh of his. He loved to laugh. He could laugh at himself, too. He was explaining a play in a meeting one day, and after he'd told us what I was supposed to do, he said, "And both blocks block. I mean, both backs black." He got all twisted, and he just broke up laughing at himself.

Some of the guys on the team used to imitate him. Vince Promuto, one of our guards, could really pick up his voice. Promuto'd say, "What in the *hell* is going on in here?" and everybody'd get scared. One day, we were getting ready to go into a meeting, and Promuto walked in the locker room and said, using that voice, "What in the *hell* is going on in here?" Everybody reached for their notebooks right away, and just then, Coach Lombardi walked in right behind Promuto and said, "Yes, what in the hell *is* going on in here?"

He used to tell us that what made football the greatest profession was that we went out and did our job even if we were hurting. He said a doctor or a lawyer, if he didn't feel well, could take a day off, but we had to go out and play on Sunday no matter how we felt. He made us proud of our injuries.

Speaking of injuries, there was a funny thing that happened with him and me. We were walking off the field one morning, and he rubbed his elbow and said, "Gee, Sonny, my elbow's really bothering me."

"Yeah?" I said. "So's mine." And I started to show him where I'd been operated on, where it hurt sometimes, and he just turned and walked away from me. "I'm not gonna listen to your problems," he said. "You're not gonna bother me with your aches and pains." It was funny as hell. He wanted some sympathy, but he wasn't about to give any.

After the season, I was visiting with him in his office, and he started talking to me about Walter Rock, one of our offensive tackles. Walter'd had some knee surgery. "You know," Coach said, "I pushed Walter Rock too hard. I pushed him and drove him and drove him and drove him. I shouldn't have done that. His knee was just completely torn up. They had to remake his knee altogether. But, you know, he came back and he played and he did the best he could. He gave it 100 per cent. I have so much respect and admiration for Walter Rock. I really like that in a man."

But, another time, just before he got sick, he said to me, "My year out of football really softened me up. It really did. I was just too easy on you guys last year. I let you all get away with too much. That's why we didn't win more games. This year, I'm gonna be tougher than I've ever been. And I'm gonna be tougher on you than on anybody else."

I understood that. I didn't mind that. I knew whatever he did to me, it'd make me a better player.

I wish he were here now, pushing me and driving me. You know what some friend of Coach Lombardi's, a

169

fellow from Chicago, said to Marie at the hospital? "God must be in a lot of trouble," he said, "if He needs Vince Lombardi."

I think I felt sorrier for Sonny than I did for any other man affected by Vince's death. He'd waited so long to be a winner. He'd waited so long to find a Vince Lombardi.

Sonny was the last man I interviewed for this book, the last man representing some 500 to 600 men that Vince had coached from 1939 through 1969.

When I left Sonny, I thought about my brief meeting with Henry Lombardi, Vince's father. We didn't really have a chance to talk. He's old and hard of hearing, and we met in the funeral home, at the wake for his oldest son. I had to repeat my name a few times before he caught it, and then he nodded and said, "Ah, Jerry Kramer."

He looked at me, and he smiled, and in an old man's voice, as though it were echoing from far away, he said, "He loved you boys. He loved you boys. He loved you boys."

SUPER BOWL SPEECH

January 14, 1968

It's very difficult for me to say anything. Anything I could say would be repetitious. This is our twenty-third game this year. I don't know of anything else I could tell this team. Boys, I can only say this to you: Boys, you're a good football team. You are a proud football team. You are the world champions. You are the champions of the National Football League for the third time in a row, for the first time in the history of the National Football League. That's a great thing to be proud of. But let me just say this: All the glory, everything that you've had, everything that you've won is going to be small in comparison to winning this one. This is a great thing for you. You're the only team maybe in the history of the National Football League to ever have this opportunity to win the Super Bowl twice. Boys, I tell you I'd be so proud of that I just fill up with myself. I just get bigger and bigger and bigger. It's not going to come easy. This is a club that's gonna hit you. They're gonna try to hit you and you got to take it out of them. You got to be forty tigers out there. That's all. Just hit. Just run. Just block and just tackle. If you do that, there's no question what the answer's going to be in this ball game. Keep your poise. Keep your poise. You've faced them all. There's nothing they can show you out there you haven't faced a number of times. Right?

HEAD COACHING RECORD

Year	Team	Won	Lost	Tied	Percentage (Excluding ties)	
1942	St. Cecilia	6	1	2	.857	
1943	St. Cecilia	11	0	0	1.000	
1944	St. Cecilia	10	0	1	1.000	
1945	St. Cecilia	5	3	2	.625	
1946	St. Cecilia	7	3	0	.700	
1959	Green Bay	7	5	0	.583	(Third place)
1960	Green Bay	8	4	0	.667	(Western champions)
1961	Green Bay	11	3	0	.786	(NFL champions)
1962	Green Bay	13	1	0	.929	(NFL champions)
1963	Green Bay	11	2	1	.846	(Second place)
1964	Green Bay	8	5	1	.615	(Second place)
1965	Green Bay	10	3	1	.769	(NFL champions)
1966	Green Bay	12	2	0	.857	(World champions)
1967	Green Bay	9	4	1	.692	(World champions)
1969	Washington	7	5	2	.583	(Second place)
	Total	135	41	11	.767	

His Green Bay teams were 42-8 in preseason games, 10-2 in postseason games.

His Washington team was 2-4 in preseason games.

His overall record: 189 victories, 55 defeats, 11 ties, .775 percentage.

From 1939 through 1941, he was an assistant at St. Cecilia High School.

From 1947 through 1948, he was an assistant at Fordham University.

From 1949 through 1953, he was an assistant at West Point.

From 1954 through 1958, he was an assistant with the New York Giants.

You never lose. But sometimes the clock runs out on you.

VINCE LOMBARDI